C000230669

RHYT
REMEMBERING

An everyday office book

Hannah Ward and Jennifer Wild

First published in Great Britain in 2013

Society for Promoting Christian Knowledge
36 Causton Street
London SW1P 4ST
www.spckpublishing.co.uk

British Library Cataloguing-in-Publication Data
A catalogue record for this book is available from the British Library

ISBN 978–0–281–07079–4
eBook ISBN 978–0–281–07080–0

Typeset by Graphicraft Limited, Hong Kong
First printed in Great Britain by Ashford Colour Press
Subsequently digitally printed in Great Britain

Contents

———◆•◆•◆———

About the authors

———————

Hannah Ward and Jennifer Wild are freelance writers and editors. Their books include *The Monastic Way*, *Resources for Preaching and Worship* (Years A, B and C), *Human Rites*, *Celebrating Women* (with Janet Morley, published by SPCK) and *Guard the Chaos*. They have both spent part of their lives as members of Anglican religious orders.

Introduction

———•◦•———

What are 'offices'? What sort of way of praying do they involve?

Offices are prayer that has been tried and tested down the ages. Although often associated with the clergy and members of religious orders, they have their origins in the early centuries when Christians gathered for communal daily prayer. This way of praying belongs to the whole church and many Christians are discovering just how rich is its tradition.

This 'everyday office book' is an invitation to try out this way of prayer if you haven't before. It may take a bit of getting used to – part of its strength is in familiarity, which takes time to build, so give it time. Another of its characteristics is a sense of rhythm. Or, at least, its potential sense of rhythm. Offices can offer a way of giving structure or pattern to a day or week – saying them at the same time, in the same place, with some of the same words, week in, week out. This is not to deny God's presence with us at all times and in all places, but offices can offer us a way of turning consciously to God at particular times of day – this is why this way of prayer is also known as the 'liturgy of the hours', and why we can talk about a 'hallowing of time'.

Offices are most usually said communally – in parish churches, cathedrals or religious communities. It may seem a little strange to be offering an office book for individual use. The fact of the matter is, though, most of us just don't have access to offices said communally. But it would be a mistake to think that if we say an office on our own, we are simply engaging in 'private' prayer. One of the great and significant characteristics of this way of praying is that it does involve a joining-in – with the wider community of the church and, more even than that, of standing together with one's fellow human beings.

This is true, we believe, even when not using an 'official' office book. Churches do, of course, have their recognized and approved prayer books, but there has always been an abundance of shorter, or specialized, versions alongside. Many Christians, whether or not they are Sunday churchgoers, find that 'saying an office' during the week makes sense. It is one way to express our prayers, our hopes and our fears. It is also a way of enacting our 'remembering' of the deeds and goodness of God, and in so doing somehow to join in that ceaseless divine activity that works for good in the world.

What we hope this book offers is a compact and easy-to-follow way of entering into this world of prayer. There are four short offices, that is, acts of worship, for every day of the week: Morning and Evening Prayer are slightly longer, but Midday and Night Prayer (the last at bedtime and also known as 'Compline') are much shorter. These two shorter offices are the same for all seasons of the year and can be found on pp. 33–58. There is also a 'Thought for the night' at the end of Night Prayer, which might offer a focus to relieve the tedium of wakefulness, or the anxieties that are never so wearying as when they keep us awake. Again, the words might not be exactly what you thought you wanted to say, but the idea is to accept them as what is 'given' on this occasion, try them out, and see what happens.

All four offices are complete as set out here – no need for a Bible, and no need to hunt round for things that lurk in other parts of the book. As well as an 'ordinary' week, there are four other weeks, intended respectively for the seasons of Advent, Christmas, Lent and Easter, so that the main 'moments' of the Christian year give their colour to the daily round, and the various rhythms of hour and day and season intertwine to enrich this act of remembrance – in its widest sense. Exactly when to use each season is up to you: most people will regard December up till Christmas Day as Advent; the Christmas season could be taken as ending after Epiphany, but could be extended as far as Candlemas on 2 February. Lent runs from Ash Wednesday to Easter Eve, Easter lasts till Pentecost, and everything unaccounted for is known as Ordinary Time.

How should this book be used? It is impossible to prescribe one thing for everyone's need, but the following may be a helpful guide:

- Individuals will find that appropriate time or times will merge for them. Try it and see. Of course, not every office has to be used every day. There is no 'has to' beyond your desire to try praying in this way.

- Inevitably, this book is all words, even though the design is intended to give a sense of spaciousness. Some people like to pray with a visible focus to help them: the act of clearing a space on the table, lighting a candle, setting up an icon or other significant picture; sitting quietly for a moment before beginning; above all, pausing at the end of each section, so that silence is the constant container of the sounds that are going on inside the head, or audibly, if one chooses to read aloud; all these and similar things serve to embody this way of praying, so that as far as possible all of oneself is involved. Even when no outward 'props' are possible (e.g. on the top of a bus) such earlier practice means that you will more easily enter into your 'space' of prayer anywhere at all.

- The material we have prepared follows broadly traditional lines; it is mostly biblical, with a few passages from later Christians, and some prayers that have been in use for many centuries – one way of keeping alive an awareness that we are only the latest in the 'great cloud of witnesses'. We have tried to ensure the presence of as many of the rich biblical images of God as possible. Some very familiar things are missing – for instance, the Lord's Prayer (except in the midday office for Sunday); and we trust that users of this book will feel free to insert anything they want to include in some appropriate place.

ORDINARY TIME

Sunday Morning Prayer

———◆·◆·◆———

Blessed are you, O God: your steadfast love endures for ever.

> God says:
> I love you often,
> because it is my nature,
> for I am Love myself.
> I love you deeply,
> because it is my desire,
> for I long for everyone to love me deeply.
> I love you long,
> because I am eternal,
> for I have no end.   *Mechthild of Magdeburg*

Blessed are you, O God: your steadfast love endures for ever.

Bless the Holy One, O my soul,
and all that is within me bless God's holy name.

Bless the Holy One, O my soul,
and forget not all God's benefits.

You forgive all our sins
and heal all our infirmities.

You redeem our life from the grave
and crown us with mercy and loving-kindness;

you execute righteousness
and judgement for all who are oppressed.
You fill our life with good things. *Psalm 103.1–4, 6*

Creator God, show us your compassion.
Redeemer Christ, show us your compassion.
Sanctifier Spirit, show us your compassion.

When the disciples had gone ashore, they saw a charcoal fire there, with fish on it, and bread. Jesus said to them, 'Bring some of that fish that you have just caught.' So Simon Peter went aboard and hauled the net ashore, full of large fish, a hundred and fifty-three of them; and though there were so many, the net was not torn. Jesus said to them, 'Come and have breakfast.' Now none of the disciples dared to ask him, 'Who are you?' because they knew it was the Lord. Jesus came and took the bread and gave it to them, and did the same with the fish. This was now the third time that Jesus appeared to the disciples after he was raised from the dead. *John 21.9–14*

Loving God,
comfort the sick
befriend the sorrowful
embrace the dying;
and guide us all to that life which has its home in you.

Love overflows into everything.
From the depths to the stars,
she surpasses all that is,
and is the most loving. *Hildegard of Bingen*

Sunday Evening Prayer

Blessed are you, O God:
in Jesus, crucified and risen, you have shown us your face.

    We worship you, O Holy One,
    present to Moses in the burning bush,
    to Isaiah in the temple,
    to John in the desert,
    to Mary at the Annunciation;
    we worship you, our Lord Jesus Christ,
    present to your disciples
    on the evening of your resurrection;
    we worship you, holy Spirit of love,
    present and dwelling in our hearts.

Blessed are you, O God:
in Jesus, crucified and risen, you have shown us your face.

Give thanks to our God, call upon the Holy One,
tell all the nations what God has done.

Sing to God, sing praises,
tell of all God's marvellous deeds.

Exult in God's holy Name,
let the hearts of those who seek our God be glad.

Seek the Most High and be strong,
seek God's face for evermore.

Psalm 105.1–4 jw

O God, when we do not know how to bear your presence,
have mercy on us and give us courage to go aside to
    meet you;
Jesus, when we are ashamed to face you in those who
    suffer,
have mercy on us, that we may see with your eyes;
Spirit of God, when we deny your presence in ourselves
    or others,
have mercy upon us and correct us with love.

On the evening of that day, the first day of the week, the doors
being locked where the disciples were, for fear of the Jews, Jesus
came and stood in their midst, and said to them, 'Peace to
you.' And saying this he showed them his hands and his side.
So then the disciples were glad at the sight of the Lord.

John 20.19–20 jw

To all who are fearful, give your peace.
To all who are lonely, give your presence.
To all who are seeking God's face, give your Spirit.

Jesus our Brother,
now and in the evening of our days,
hold us in your presence,
that we may keep to your truth,
suffer with your courage
and love with your love.

Monday Morning Prayer

Blessed are you, O God,
   source of all wisdom and understanding.

O powerful Wisdom,
you encircle all that is,
holding everything together
in one life-giving path.   *Hildegard of Bingen*

Blessed are you, O God,
   source of all wisdom and understanding.

O God, you are my God; eagerly I seek you;
my soul thirsts for you, my flesh faints for you,
   as in a barren and dry land where there is no water;

therefore I have gazed upon you in your holy place,
that I might behold your power and your glory.

For your loving-kindness is better than life itself;
my lips shall give you praise.

So will I bless you as long as I live
and lift up my hands in your name.   *Psalm 63.1–4*

Creator God, show us your compassion.
Redeemer Christ, show us your compassion.
Sanctifier Spirit, show us your compassion.

Wisdom is radiant and unfading,
and she is easily discerned by those who love her,
and is found by those who seek her.
She hastens to make herself known to those who desire her.
One who rises early to seek her will have no difficulty,
for she will be found sitting at the gate.
To fix one's thought on her is perfect understanding,
and one who is vigilant on her account will soon be free
   from care,
because she goes about seeking those worthy of her,
and she graciously appears to them in their paths,
and meets them in every thought.   *Wisdom 6.12–16*

To all who try to understand the workings of your universe,
give a clear mind and a sense of wonder;
to those who teach and those who learn,
give a thirst for knowledge
and an acceptance of what cannot be known;
to all who seek discernment of your ways,
give a firm faith and simple trust.

With you, our God, are wisdom and strength,
   counsel and understanding;
we praise you, now and for ever. Amen.

Monday Evening Prayer

Blessed be God, who has shown us light.

> Let us worship the God of our salvation:
> to you, O God, be praise.
> Jesus Christ, Saviour of the world:
> to you, O Christ, be praise.
> Holy Spirit of God, light of our being:
> to you, our God, be praise.

Blessed be God, who has shown us light.

A lamp for my feet is your law,
and light for my steps.

I have solemnly sworn
to keep your righteous judgements.

I am brought very low:
God, give me life, according to your word.

Accept the willing offerings of my lips
and teach me your judgements.   *Psalm 119.105–108 JW*

> Where we have turned away from you, Lord,
> be a lamp to light our way home:
> *Lord, have mercy.*
> Where we have brought suffering on others,
> teach us true justice:
> *Christ, have mercy.*

Direct our hearts in your ways;
renew your life in us:
Lord, have mercy.

You are the world's light. A city cannot be hidden if it is built
on a hill. No one after lighting a lamp puts it under the bushel
measure, but on the lampstand, and it gives light to the whole
household. In the same way, let your light shine before others,
so that they may see your good deeds and give glory to your
Father in heaven.   *Matthew 5.14–16 jw*

For all people of faith:
may they be light in the world.
For those in the darkness of sickness, hunger, or conflict:
bring them new life in your presence.
For all who have lost their way:
be a light to their paths.
For all who exploit others:
show them your righteous judgements.
For ourselves at the end of the day:
show us your face, O God.

For you, our God,
are good and loving to everyone,
and we glorify you,
the light of our lives,
now and for ever.
Amen.

Tuesday Morning Prayer

Blessed are you, O God, giver of life to all things.

> The Holy Spirit –
> life that enlivens,
> energizing everything,
> root of all creaturely life.
> And all is made good,
> offences wiped clean,
> wounds tended.
> This is life alight,
> worthy of praise,
> life that awakens
> and re-awakens
> everything.   *Hildegard of Bingen*

Blessed are you, O God, giver of life to all things.

I waited patiently upon you, O God;
you stooped to me and heard my cry.

You lifted me out of the desolate pit, out of the mire and clay;
you set my feet upon a high cliff, and made my footing sure.

You put a new song in my mouth, a song of praise to our God;
many shall see and stand in awe and put their trust in you.

Psalm 40.1–4

> Creator God, show us your compassion.
> Redeemer Christ, show us your compassion.
> Sanctifier Spirit, show us your compassion.

Surely, this commandment that I am commanding you today is not too hard for you, nor is it too far away. It is not in heaven, that you should say, 'Who will go up to heaven for us, and get it for us so that we may hear it and observe it?' Neither is it beyond the sea, that you should say, 'Who will cross to the other side of the sea for us, and get it for us so that we may hear it and observe it?' No, the word is very near to you; it is in your mouth and in your heart for you to observe.

See, I have set before you today life and prosperity, death and adversity . . . Choose life so that you and your descendants may live, loving the Lord your God.   *Deuteronomy 30.11–15, 19b–20a*

For the earth and its creatures,
I choose life.
For prisoners and those who seek asylum,
I choose life.
For my friends and family,
I choose life.
For those I find it hard to love,
I choose life.
Today, O God, in everything I do,
I choose life.

Breath of Life,
breathe through your creation;
renew our spirits,
refresh our minds,
and lead us to our home in you.

Tuesday Evening Prayer

Blessed be God, holy and undivided Trinity,
our hope, our refuge, and our advocate!

> God, our stronghold, our place of safety:
> you are our rock and our strength.
> Jesus, yokefellow,
> you are our companion on the way.
> Holy Breath of God, yours is the life in us,
> and the life to which we are called.

Blessed be God, holy and undivided Trinity,
our hope, our refuge, and our advocate!

O God, heaven is the height of your mercy
and your truth reaches as far as the clouds;

your righteousness is like your mountains,
your judgements like a bottomless abyss.

Your people will put their hope in the shelter of your wings;
they will be intoxicated with the riches of your house,

and you will give them drink from your pleasures
like a river in flood.

For with you is the wellspring of life,
and in your light shall we see light.   *Psalm 36.5–6, 7b–9 jw*

Lord, our refuge, in my own heart I have seen
the wickedness of those who despise you:
  Lord, have mercy.
Jesus, companion, you offer your humble yoke
to those who like to hold their heads high:
  Christ, have mercy.
Spirit of wisdom, cleanse the thoughts of my heart,
the words of my lips, the deeds that I do:
  Lord, have mercy.

Everyone who hears these words of mine, and does them, I say that that person will be like a wise man who built his house on rock; and the rain fell and the rivers flooded and the winds blew, and they fell upon that house, but the house did not fall, because its foundations were on rock. And everyone who hears these words of mine, and does not do them, I say that that person will be like a foolish man, who built his house on sand; and the rain fell and the rivers flooded and the winds blew, and they struck that house, and it fell; and its fall was a mighty one.   *Matthew 7.24–27 jw*

God our Rock and Refuge,
guard all peoples tenderly while you open their eyes
  to see what is truly wise;
  to reject dishonesty in word and deed;
  and to reach out always towards the good.
Gracious and generous Giver, expand the hearts of all peoples
  to be grateful for the abundance of your gifts;
  to share resources willingly;
  and to rejoice in both giving and receiving from each other.

To you, our God,
our Shelter from the stresses of the day
and Protector from night's fears,
we make our evening offering of praise,
as is your due and our delight.
In your own name we pray. Amen.

Wednesday Morning Prayer

Blessed be God,
   bringer of justice for the orphan and oppressed.

Let justice roll down like waters,
   and righteousness like an ever-flowing stream.   *Amos 5.24*

Blessed be God,
   bringer of justice for the orphan and oppressed.

Happy are they who have the God of Jacob for their help,
whose hope is in their God;

who made heaven and earth, the seas and all that is in them;
who keeps a promise for ever;

who gives justice to those who are oppressed,
and food to those who hunger.

Our God sets the prisoners free, and opens the eyes of the
   blind;
our God lifts up those who are bowed down.   *Psalm 146.4–7*

   Creator God, show us your compassion.
   Redeemer Christ, show us your compassion.
   Sanctifier Spirit, show us your compassion.

Many crowds followed Jesus, and he cured all of them, and he ordered them not to make him known. This was to fulfil what had been spoken through the prophet Isaiah:

'Here is my servant, whom I have chosen,
  my beloved, with whom my soul is well pleased.
I will put my Spirit upon him,
  and he will proclaim justice to the Gentiles.
He will not wrangle or cry aloud,
  nor will anyone hear his voice in the streets.
He will not break a bruised reed
  or quench a smouldering wick
until he brings justice to victory.
  And in his name the Gentiles will hope.'   *Matthew 12.15b–21*

Where there is war and hatred,
let there be peace.
Where there is hunger and nakedness,
let there be plenty.
Where there is bondage and slavery,
let there be freedom.

Give to all your people, O God,
that dignity which reflects your glory,
Creator, Redeemer and Sanctifier.
Amen.

Wednesday Evening Prayer

Blessed are you, O God,
God of all the ages, and of all creatures.

> Blessed is your unfailing love towards us,
> to those before us, and all who will come after us,
> seeking your peace and your righteousness:
> with thankfulness we turn to you,
> our Maker, our Redeemer, our Sanctifier,
> holy and life-giving Trinity.

Blessed are you, O God,
God of all the ages, and of all creatures.

O God, listen to my prayer,
in your faithfulness attend to my entreaties;
hear me in your righteousness.

Do not enter into judgement with your servant,
for no one living is righteous in your sight.

For my enemy has brought my life down to the ground,
and made me sit in darkness like those long dead.

And so my spirit is weak within me;
my heart within me is distressed.

I remember old times, I go over all your deeds,
I meditate on the works of your hands.   *Psalm 143.1–5 JW*

Mindful of our sins, and the sins of many,
we cry to you, Searcher of hearts and minds:
   Lord, have mercy.
Mindful of the pains and griefs we have caused, or suffered,
we cry to you, Man of Sorrows:
   Christ, have mercy.
Mindful of your work in us, and in all creation,
we cry to you, Treasury of blessings and life-giver:
   Lord, have mercy.

Remember Jesus Christ raised from the dead, Jesus, David's
descendant. This is the good news I preach, for which I suffer
distress, to the point of being fettered like a wrongdoer. But
God's word is not fettered. So I put up with everything for the
sake of the elect, so that they also may win the salvation that
is in Christ Jesus, with eternal glory.   *2 Timothy 2.8–11 JW*

God, of your goodness grant
   to the despairing, hope;
   to the suffering, endurance;
   to the dying, your presence;
   to all who long for it, the salvation that is in Christ Jesus;
   to all your holy ones, the eternal weight of glory.

Let all the ends of the earth remember and return
to you, our God;
let all the nations worship before you –
you who alone are undying,
dwelling in light unapproachable,
you no one has ever seen or can see;
to you be honour and dominion for ever.

                                        Last four lines 1 Timothy 6.16 JW

Thursday Morning Prayer

Blessed are you, O God: you give in abundance.

> You spread a table before me
> in the presence of those who trouble me;
> you have anointed my head with oil,
> and my cup is running over. *Psalm 23.5*

Blessed are you, O God: you give in abundance.

The eyes of all wait upon you, O God,
and you give them their food in due season.

You open wide your hand
and satisfy the needs of every living creature.

You are righteous in all your ways
and loving in all your works.

You are near to those who call upon you,
to all who call upon you faithfully.

You fulfil the desire of those who fear you,
you hear their cry and help them. *Psalm 145.16–20*

> Creator God, show us your compassion.
> Redeeming Christ, show us your compassion.
> Sanctifier Spirit, show us your compassion.

The kingdom of heaven is like a landowner who went out early in the morning to hire labourers for his vineyard. After agreeing with the labourers for the usual daily wage, he sent them into his vineyard. When he went out about nine o'clock, he saw others standing idle in the market-place; and he said to them, 'You also go into the vineyard, and I will pay you whatever is right.' So they went. When he went out again at about noon and about three o'clock, he did the same. And about five o'clock . . . When evening came, the owner of the vineyard said to his manager, 'Call the labourers and give them their pay, beginning with the last and then going to the first.' When those hired about five o'clock came, each of them received the usual daily wage. Now when the first came, they thought they would receive more; but each of them also received the usual daily wage. And when they received it, they grumbled against the landowner, saying, 'These last worked only one hour, and you have made them equal to us who have borne the burden of the day and the scorching heat.' But he replied to one of them, 'Friend, I am doing you no wrong; did you not agree with me for the usual daily wage? Take what belongs to you and go; I choose to give to this last the same as I give to you. Am I not allowed to do what I choose with what belongs to me? Or are you envious because I am generous?' So the last will be first, and the first will be last. *Matthew 20.1–16*

Generous God,
we thank you for the abundance of your riches.
Keep us from meanness of spirit,
and give us big enough hearts to rejoice with others
in their good fortune.

Immortal love, forever full,
Forever flowing free,
Forever shared, forever whole,
A never-ebbing sea!   *John G. Whittier*

Thursday Evening Prayer

Blessed are you, O God:
you open your hands, and fill all things with plenteousness.

We bless you, generous God:
you show us how to give and to receive.
Jesus our brother, you make your presence known among us
in the breaking of the bread,
and in the stranger who comes to us in need.
We worship you, Holy Spirit of God,
inspirer of all that is good.

Blessed are you, O God:
you open your hands, and fill all things with plenteousness.

I am God, your God,
who brought you up out of the land of Egypt.
Open your mouth wide, and I will fill it.

But my people did not listen to my voice,
and Israel did not heed me.

If only my people would listen to me,
if only Israel would walk in my ways!

I would feed you with the finest wheat,
and with honey from the rock I would satisfy you.

Psalm 81.10–11, 13, 16 jw

From our blinkered vision, O God,
    set us free to see as you do.
From our suspicious fears, Jesus,
    rouse us up to follow your way.
From our laziness and backsliding, Holy Spirit,
    stir us up to real life.

May the God of patient endurance and encouragement grant you to be of one mind among yourselves, in accord with Christ Jesus, so that together you may, as one, glorify the God and Father of our Lord Jesus Christ. Welcome each other, therefore, just as Christ has welcomed you, for the glory of God.   *Romans 15.5–7 JW*

May we all find our part to play so that
the hungry may be fed,
the homeless find shelter,
the lonely be comforted,
the persecuted find relief,
and the fainthearted courage.

You must sit down, says Love, and taste my meat:
So I did sit and eat.   *George Herbert*

Friday Morning Prayer

Blessed are you, O God,
  for by your wounds we have been healed.

  Blessed be Jesus, friend and brother,
  sharer of our humanity,
  suffering One who knows our pain.
  You are our hope,
  our comfort
  and our redeemer.

Blessed are you, O God,
  for by your wounds we have been healed.

Happy are they who consider the poor and needy!
God will deliver them in the time of trouble.

You, O God, preserve them and keep them alive,
  so that they may be happy in the land;
you do not hand them over to the will of their enemies.

You sustain them on their sick-bed:
and minister to them in their illness.

I said, 'Be merciful to me, O God;
heal me, for I have sinned against you.'   *Psalm 41.1–4*

  Creator God, show us your compassion.
  Redeemer Christ, show us your compassion.
  Sanctifier Spirit, show us your compassion.

Jesus called the twelve together and gave them power and authority over all demons and to cure diseases, and he sent them out to proclaim the kingdom of God and to heal. He said to them, 'Take nothing for your journey, no staff, nor bag, nor bread, nor money – not even an extra tunic. Whatever house you enter, stay there, and leave from there. Wherever they do not welcome you, as you are leaving that town shake the dust off your feet as a testimony against them.' They departed and went through the villages, bringing the good news and curing diseases everywhere. *Luke 9.1–6*

To the lonely and rejected
Come, Lord Jesus.
To the frightened and anxious
Come, Lord Jesus.
To the sick and dying
Come, Lord Jesus.
To broken communities and war-torn countries
Come, Lord Jesus.

Come, Lord Jesus,
to all who cry out in anguish.
Heal us, restore us, and grant us life eternal.
Amen.

Friday Evening Prayer

Blessed are you, O God: your work is perfect.

For your wonderful creation, we praise you, our Maker.
For the labour of redemption, we thank you,
   Jesus our saviour.
For your life-giving energy, we glorify you, Spirit of God.
Holy Three in One: we worship you.

Blessed are you, O God: your work is perfect.

Great is your work, and worthy of all praise, O God,
and your righteousness endures for ever and ever.

Memorable are your wonderful deeds;
O God, you are gracious and merciful.

You have sent redemption to your people;
you have commanded your covenant for ever;
your Name is holy and revered.

The fear of you is the beginning of wisdom;
all those who practise it have a good understanding;
your praise endures for ever and ever.   *Psalm 111.3–4, 9–10 JW*

O God, what are we humans, that you are mindful of us?
 Lord, have mercy.
Lord Jesus, when we were far off, you brought us near:
 Christ, have mercy.
Spirit of God, work the work of your transforming love in us:
 Lord, have mercy.

Jesus said to them, 'Truly, truly, I tell you, the Son can do nothing of himself, but only what he sees the Father doing; for whatever the Father does, this the Son does likewise. For the Father loves the Son and shows him everything that he himself is doing; and he will show him greater works than these, which will amaze you. For just as the Father raises the dead and gives them life, so also the Son gives life to whomever he wishes.

John 5.19–21 jw

Lord Jesus,
worker of the world's salvation,
fill the world
with love's energy,
love's endurance
and love's endless inventiveness.

And may you who at this hour lay in the tomb
revive in us your indestructible life
to the glory of God.
Amen.

Saturday Morning Prayer

Blessed are you, O God:
you renew us with your goodness and loving-kindness.

> New every morning is the love
> Our wakening and uprising prove;
> Through sleep and darkness safely brought,
> Restored to life and power and thought.   *John Keble*

Blessed are you, O God:
you renew us with your goodness and loving-kindness.

Be joyful in God, all you lands;
sing the glory of God's name;
    sing the glory of God's praise.

Say to God, 'How awesome are your deeds!
Because of your great strength
    your enemies cringe before you.

'All the earth bows down before you,
sings to you, sings out your name.'

Come now and see the works of God,
how wonderful you are in your doing towards all people.

Bless our God, you peoples,
make the voice of God's praise to be heard;

who holds our souls in life,
and will not allow our feet to slip.   *Psalm 66.1–4, 7–8*

Creator God, show us your compassion.
Redeeming Christ, show us your compassion.
Sanctifier Spirit, show us your compassion.

Jesus told them a parable: 'No one tears a piece from a new garment and sews it on an old garment; otherwise the new will be torn, and the piece from the new will not match the old. And no one puts new wine into old wineskins; otherwise the new wine will burst the skins and will be spilled, and the skins will be destroyed. But new wine must be put into fresh wineskins.'   *Luke 5.36–38*

Maker God,
we pray for those confused by change;
for those whose memories are fading
and for all who are afraid of the future.
As you call us to newness of life,
help us both to cherish the past
and to reach out towards the unknown.

I am about to do a new thing;
    now it springs forth, do you not perceive it?   *Isaiah 43.19a*

Saturday Evening Prayer

Blessed are you, O God, Maker of all:
in Jesus Christ you offer everlasting newness of life.

New life demands a new song,
the song of the kingdom of heaven.
Not just our lips but our lives
are to sing every day
the wordless song of the thankful heart
with love, to you, our God.

Blessed are you, O God, Maker of all:
in Jesus Christ you offer everlasting newness of life.

How manifold are your works, O God!
How wisely you have made every one of them!
The earth is filled with your making!

Here is the sea, this vast expanse,
filled with creeping things without number –
living beings, small and large together.

There go the ships to and fro,
and Leviathan, whom you fashioned as a playfellow.

All of them look to you expectantly,
to provide their food when they need it.

You open your hand – the whole creation is satisfied
    with your bounty.
You take away their breath – they die and revert to dust.

You breathe forth your breath – they come into being,
and you renew the face of the earth.   *Psalm 104.24–28, 29b–30 JW*

When I am impatient,
calm me down.
When I am choosy,
make me laugh at myself.
When I think I have nothing to give,
remind me of the next small thing
and, above all,
let me remember
that I am just one of your creatures,
and thank you.

With you, my God, is wisdom – she knows your works and she
was present when you made the cosmos, she understands what
is pleasing in your eyes and what is right in accordance with
your commandments. Send her out from the holy heavens, send
her from your glorious throne, that she may labour alongside
me and that I may know what is acceptable to you.

Wisdom 9.9–10 JW

For all artists, scientists, students and teachers,
for parents and children,
for politicians and thinkers,
for leaders and followers,
for visionaries and dreamers,
for friends and neighbours,
for those in health and those in sickness,
for all of us, old and young,
in our daily work and living,
for all of humankind,

that we may grow into the measure
of the full stature of Christ
to the glory of you, our God and Maker.

For God's goodness comprehends all his creatures and all his blessed works and overpasses them without end.

Julian of Norwich

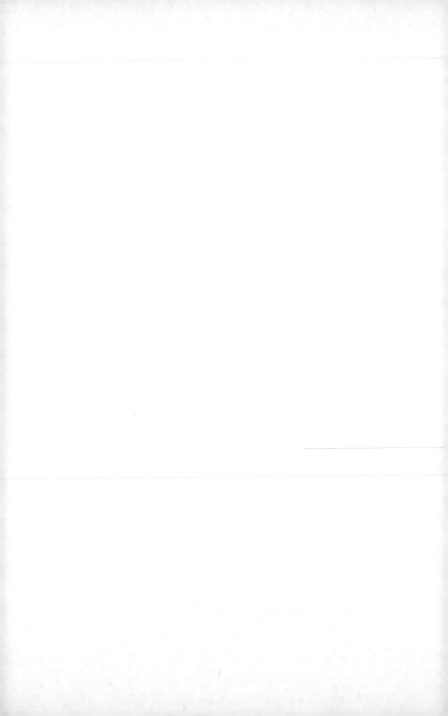

MIDDAY AND NIGHT PRAYER FOR ALL SEASONS

Sunday Midday Prayer

This is the day that the Lord has made:
we will rejoice and be glad in it.

Blessed are the poor in spirit, for theirs is
the kingdom of heaven.

We will honour them.

Blessed are those who mourn, for they will be comforted.

We will listen to them.

Blessed are the meek, for they will inherit the earth.

We will imitate them.

Blessed are those who hunger and thirst for righteousness,
for they will be filled.

We will struggle for them.

Blessed are the merciful, for they will receive mercy.

Matthew 5.3–7

We will be led by them,
until we come with them to the eternal kingdom
where the blessed reign with God,
world without end.
Amen.

Sunday Night Prayer

May the Lord grant us a quiet night and a perfect end.

> For all the good I have seen and done today, I give thanks.
> For all my sins and omissions, I ask pardon.
> For all for whom I pray, I claim protection.

If you dwell under the shelter of the Most High,
and abide in the shadow of the God of heaven,

you need not be afraid of any terror of the night
or the trouble that goes about in the darkness.

God says, 'Those who love me, I will rescue,
I will protect those who know my name.

When they call out to me, I will answer them,
I will be with them in trouble,
I will deliver them and treat them with honour;

with length of days I will satisfy them,
and I will show them my salvation.'   *Psalm 91.1, 5a, 6a, 14–16 JW*

In peace I will lie down and sleep;
for you alone, O God, make me dwell in confidence.

Master, now you are letting your servant go,
according to your word, in peace;

for my own eyes have seen your salvation,
which you have prepared in the sight of all peoples,

a light of revelation for the nations,
and glory for your people Israel.   *Luke 2.29–32 JW*

In peace I will lie down and sleep;
for you alone, O God, make me dwell in confidence.

    Protect us through this night,
    that we may sleep in peace
    and wake refreshed to greet the new day.

*

'Be still and know that I am God.'

Monday Midday Prayer

Open to me the gates of righteousness:
I will enter and give thanks to the Lord.

Blessed are the pure in heart, for they will see God.

Grant us single-heartedness.

Blessed are the peacemakers, for they will be called
   children of God.

Grant us to fight for peace with justice.

Blessed are those who are persecuted for righteousness'
   sake, for theirs is the kingdom of heaven.

Grant us to stand alongside the persecuted.

Blessed are you when people revile you and persecute you
and utter all kinds of evil against you falsely on my account.
Rejoice and be glad, for your reward is great in heaven, for
in the same way they persecuted the prophets who were
before you.   *Matthew 5.8–12*

   Grant us to come with all the blessed
   to that eternal kingdom,
   where we shall see you face to face.
   Amen.

Monday Night Prayer

Every night I will bless you: and praise your name for ever.

> For all the good I have seen and done today, I give thanks.
> For all my sins and omissions, I ask pardon.
> For all for whom I pray, I claim protection.

If you dwell under the shelter of the Most High,
and abide in the shadow of the God of heaven,

you need not be afraid of any terror of the night
or the trouble that goes about in the darkness.

God says, 'Those who love me, I will rescue,
I will protect those who know my name.

When they call out to me, I will answer them,
I will be with them in trouble,
I will deliver them and treat them with honour;

with length of days I will satisfy them,
and I will show them my salvation.' *Psalm 91.1, 5a, 6a, 14–16 JW*

In peace I will lie down and sleep;
for you alone, O God, make me dwell in confidence.

Master, now you are letting your servant go,
according to your word, in peace;

for my own eyes have seen your salvation,
which you have prepared in the sight of all peoples,

a light of revelation for the nations,
and glory for your people Israel.   *Luke 2.29–32 JW*

In peace I will lie down and sleep;
for you alone, O God, make me dwell in confidence.

   Be with us through night's darkness;
   banish our fears and still our minds,
   for darkness and light are both alike to you.

*

In the night your song is with me.

Tuesday Midday Prayer

Our God lives!
Blessed be my rock, and praised be the God of my salvation.

Blessed are you, O Lord our God,
for you have come to your people and set them free.

*Deliver those who today struggle with poverty, sickness or
injustice.*

You have raised up for us a mighty Saviour
in the family of David your servant.

Save us from the consequences of our sins and weaknesses.

Through the mouth of your holy prophets of old
you promised
that you would save us from our enemies,
and from the hand of all who hate us.

*Show us how to meet hostility with calmness and fair
judgement.*

You promised to show mercy to our ancestors,
and to remember your holy covenant –

*Draw together into the fellowship of love those who are
divided by envy, fear and suspicion.*

the oath that you swore to our father Abraham,
that you would set us free from the hand of our enemies,

Lead those who look to Abraham as father of the faithful
  more and more into mutual understanding.

to worship you without fear,
  in holiness and righteousness before you,
all the days of our life.   *Luke 1.68–75 JW*

  Give your wisdom to all who seek you,
  that they may find you and serve you as you deserve,
  for you are God of all times and all peoples,
  today and always.
  Amen.

Tuesday Night Prayer

May the peace of the Lord be with us this night.

For all the good I have seen and done today, I give thanks.
For all my sins and omissions, I ask pardon.
For all for whom I pray, I claim protection.

If you dwell under the shelter of the Most High,
and abide in the shadow of the God of heaven,

you need not be afraid of any terror of the night
or the trouble that goes about in the darkness.

God says, 'Those who love me, I will rescue,
I will protect those who know my name.

When they call out to me, I will answer them,
I will be with them in trouble,
I will deliver them and treat them with honour;

with length of days I will satisfy them,
and I will show them my salvation.'   *Psalm 91.1, 5a, 6a, 14–16 JW*

In peace I will lie down and sleep;
for you alone, O God, make me dwell in confidence.

Master, now you are letting your servant go,
according to your word, in peace;

for my own eyes have seen your salvation,
which you have prepared in the sight of all peoples,

a light of revelation for the nations,
and glory for your people Israel.   *Luke 2.29–32 JW*

In peace I will lie down and sleep;
for you alone, O God, make me dwell in confidence.

   I will not lie down with evil,
   Nor shall evil lie down with me,
   But I will lie down with God,
   And God will lie down with me.   *Carmina Gadelica*

*

Abide in my love.

Wednesday Midday Prayer

Open my lips, O Lord:
and my mouth shall declare your praise.

You, child, will be called the prophet of the Most High,
for you will go before the face of God to prepare the way,

Let those who claim to speak in your name, speak worthily
    of you.

to give knowledge of salvation to God's people,
by the forgiveness of all their sins.

Let those who hear your word know the awareness of sin
    and the joy of your welcoming love.

Through the tender compassion of our God,
the dawn from on high will break upon us,

Let those who are near to despair find hope.

to shine on those who sit in darkness
    and the shadow of death,
and to guide our feet into the way of peace.   *Luke 1.76–79 jw*

Comfort the dying,
welcome those who have died this day,
draw us all more and more
   into the ways of your peaceable kingdom
where you are alive and reign today and always.
Amen.

Wednesday Night Prayer

Return, O my soul, to your rest,
for the Lord has dealt bountifully with you.   *Psalm 116.7*

For all the good I have seen and done today, I give thanks.
For all my sins and omissions, I ask pardon.
For all for whom I pray, I claim protection.

If you dwell under the shelter of the Most High,
and abide in the shadow of the God of heaven,

you need not be afraid of any terror of the night
or the trouble that goes about in the darkness.

God says, 'Those who love me, I will rescue,
I will protect those who know my name.

When they call out to me, I will answer them,
I will be with them in trouble,
I will deliver them and treat them with honour;

with length of days I will satisfy them,
and I will show them my salvation.'   *Psalm 91.1, 5a, 6a, 14–16 jw*

In peace I will lie down and sleep;
for you alone, O God, make me dwell in confidence.

Master, now you are letting your servant go,
according to your word, in peace;

for my own eyes have seen your salvation,
which you have prepared in the sight of all peoples,

a light of revelation for the nations,
and glory for your people Israel.   *Luke 2.29–32 JW*

In peace I will lie down and sleep;
for you alone, O God, make me dwell in confidence.

   The sacred Three to save, to shield, to surround
   the hearth, the house, the household,
   this eve, this night and every night, each single night. Amen.
                                              Carmina Gadelica

                                   *

   Answer me when I call, O God of my righteousness.

Thursday Midday Prayer

Sing for joy, O heavens, and exalt, O earth:
break forth, O mountains, into singing!

My soul declares the greatness of the Lord,
my spirit rejoices in God my saviour;

For the dance of all creation, all praise and thanks to you.

O God, you have looked with favour on your lowly servant.
See, from now on all generations will call me blessed,

For the gifts of life and love, all praise and thanks to you.

for you, O Most Mighty, have done great things for me:
and holy is your name;

For the beauty of your saints, all praise and thanks to you.

and you have mercy on one generation after another
of those who fear you.   *Luke 1.46–50 JW*

For your tender and enduring compassion,
all praise and thanks to you.
All praise and thanks to God,
Creator, Redeemer and Sustainer.
Amen.

Thursday Night Prayer

The Lord says,
'Pause and be quiet, my people, because your rest will come.'

2 Esdras 2.24

For all the good I have seen and done today, I give thanks.
For all my sins and omissions, I ask pardon.
For all for whom I pray, I claim protection.

If you dwell under the shelter of the Most High,
and abide in the shadow of the God of heaven,

you need not be afraid of any terror of the night
or the trouble that goes about in the darkness.

God says, 'Those who love me, I will rescue,
I will protect those who know my name.

When they call out to me, I will answer them,
I will be with them in trouble,
I will deliver them and treat them with honour;

with length of days I will satisfy them,
and I will show them my salvation.'   *Psalm 91.1, 5a, 6a, 14–16 JW*

In peace I will lie down and sleep;
for you alone, O God, make me dwell in confidence.

Master, now you are letting your servant go,
according to your word, in peace;

for my own eyes have seen your salvation,
which you have prepared in the sight of all peoples,

a light of revelation for the nations,
and glory for your people Israel.   *Luke 2.29–32 JW*

In peace I will lie down and sleep;
for you alone, O God, make me dwell in confidence.

Take from us, merciful God,
the worries and weariness of this day,
that we may find our place of rest
in the sure embrace of your eternal love.

*

Do not let your heart be troubled.

Friday Midday Prayer

It is God who girds me with strength
and sets me secure on the heights.

You have shown the strength of your arm,
you have scattered the proud in their hearts' imaginings.

*Give compassionate hearts to those who lead
and exercise authority over us.*

You have brought down the mighty from their thrones,
and have raised up the oppressed.

*Infuse with your strength and power the despised,
rejected and downtrodden.*

The hungry you have filled with good things,
and the rich you have sent away empty.

Sustain all who suffer want and neglect.

You have come to the help of your people,
remembering your mercy,

Embrace the lonely, the bereaved, and all who cry out in pain.

as you promised our ancestors,
Abraham and his children for ever.   *Luke 1.51–55 JW*

Keep faith with us,
that we may keep faith with you,
today and always. Amen.

Friday Night Prayer

O Lord my God, my Saviour, by day and night I pray to you.

For all the good I have seen and done today, I give thanks.
For all my sins and omissions, I ask pardon.
For all for whom I pray, I claim protection.

If you dwell under the shelter of the Most High,
and abide in the shadow of the God of heaven,

you need not be afraid of any terror of the night
or the trouble that goes about in the darkness.

God says, 'Those who love me, I will rescue,
I will protect those who know my name.

When they call out to me, I will answer them,
I will be with them in trouble,
I will deliver them and treat them with honour;

with length of days I will satisfy them,
and I will show them my salvation.'   *Psalm 91.1, 5a, 6a, 14–16 JW*

In peace I will lie down and sleep;
for you alone, O God, make me dwell in confidence.

Master, now you are letting your servant go,
according to your word, in peace;

for my own eyes have seen your salvation,
which you have prepared in the sight of all peoples,

a light of revelation for the nations,
and glory for your people Israel.   *Luke 2.29–32 jw*

In peace I will lie down and sleep;
for you alone, O God, make me dwell in confidence.

Merciful One, bring your own radiance to this night
and protect us from all that hides
from the light of your love.

*

For you alone my soul waits in silence.

Saturday Midday Prayer

God said: When you call upon me I will answer you.
I will be with you in trouble, and I will deliver you.

Our Father in heaven,
for you love all your creation

hallowed be your name,
for your nature and your name is love

your kingdom come,
for your kingdom is a righteous kingdom

your will be done,
for your will is all that is good and perfect and acceptable

on earth as in heaven.
for your holy nature must be manifested here and hereafter

Give us today our daily bread.
for the world needs bread, the bread of your presence

Forgive us our sins
for without you we cannot begin to love

as we forgive those who sin against us.
for we are changed into the likeness of Jesus, the Human One

Lead us not into temptation
for without you we are not able to stand upright

But deliver us from evil.
for you alone are the Holy One

For the kingdom, the power, and the glory are yours
now and for ever. Amen.

Saturday Night Prayer

In returning and rest you shall be saved;
in quietness and in trust shall be your strength.   *Isaiah 30.15*

For all the good I have seen and done today, I give thanks.
For all my sins and omissions, I ask pardon.
For all for whom I pray, I claim protection.

If you dwell under the shelter of the Most High,
and abide in the shadow of the God of heaven,

you need not be afraid of any terror of the night
or the trouble that goes about in the darkness.

God says, 'Those who love me, I will rescue,
I will protect those who know my name.

When they call out to me, I will answer them,
I will be with them in trouble,
I will deliver them and treat them with honour;

with length of days I will satisfy them,
and I will show them my salvation.'   *Psalm 91.1, 5a, 6a, 14–16 JW*

In peace I will lie down and sleep;
for you alone, O God, make me dwell in confidence.

Master, now you are letting your servant go,
according to your word, in peace;

for my own eyes have seen your salvation,
which you have prepared in the sight of all peoples,

a light of revelation for the nations,
and glory for your people Israel.   *Luke 2.29–32 jw*

In peace I will lie down and sleep;
for you alone, O God, make me dwell in confidence.

Christ with me sleeping,
Christ with me waking,
Christ with me watching, every day and night.   *Carmina Gadelica*

*

Abide in my love.

ADVENT

Sunday Morning Prayer

O God, you are my God; eagerly I seek you.

O that you would tear open the heavens and come down,
so that the mountains would quake at your presence –
as when fire kindles brushwood
and the fire causes water to boil –
to make your name known to your adversaries
so that the nations might tremble at your presence!

Isaiah 64.1–2

O God, you are my God; eagerly I seek you.

I lift up my eyes to the hills;
from where is my help to come?

My help comes from God,
the maker of heaven and earth.

God will not let your foot be moved,
the One who watches over you will not fall asleep.

God will preserve you from all evil;
the Most High keep you safe.

Psalm 121.1–3, 7

In weakness,
in smallness of hope, in vulnerable faith,
we come in penitence
and await your renewing Spirit. *Dorothy McRae-McMahon*

There was a man sent from God, whose name was John. He came as a witness to testify to the light, so that all might believe through him. He himself was not the light, but he came to testify to the light. The true light, which enlightens everyone, was coming into the world. *John 1.6–9*

Promised One,
come to those whose need is great.
Heal the sick,
restore the dispirited
and embrace the dying.

For all under heaven who will come there, their way is by longing and desire. *Julian of Norwich*

Sunday Evening Prayer

We look for you, O God: we wait for you,
we long for your deliverance.

   O God, you summon us to come to you –
   We beg you, come to us!
   In Jesus Christ we encounter you –
   Come, Lord Jesus!

We look for you, O God: we wait for you,
we long for your deliverance.

O God, what are human beings, that you care for us?
The human race, that you take account of us?

Without you our lives are empty,
our days passing by like so many shadows.

Dear God, split the heavens open and come down!
Touch the mountains, and they will smoke;

let your lightning strike and dispel them.
Stretch out your hand and scatter them.

Rescue us from deep waters,
and we will sing and play for you a new song.

Psalm 144.3–7a, 9 jw

Loving God, sweep aside our anxious fears:
have mercy, forgive us.
Jesus, Son of God, come to meet us:
have mercy, forgive us.
Spirit of God, breathe new life into our lives:
have mercy, forgive us.

And he showed me the river of the water of life, shining like crystal, coming forth from the throne of God and of the Lamb. In the midst of the open space of the city, and on either side of the river, is the tree of life that bears twelve fruits, yielding its fruit every month, and the leaves of the tree are for the healing of the nations. And nothing unclean is there at all. And the throne of God and the Lamb will be there in it, and God's servants will worship him and see his face, and God's name will be on their foreheads. And there will no longer be night; they no longer have need of light of lamp or of sun, for the Lord God will be their light, and they will reign for ever and ever.   *Revelation 22.1–5 jw*

For the healing of the nations, come, Lord Jesus!
For the comfort of the outcast, come, Lord Jesus!
For the rousing of the churches, come, Lord Jesus!

O Wisdom, you came forth from the mouth of the Most High, and you reach from one end of creation to the other, ordering all things mightily and sweetly: come, and teach us the way of prudence!   *Traditional*

Monday Morning Prayer

Blessed be God: our hope is in you.

> God shall judge between the nations,
>   and shall arbitrate for many peoples;
> they shall beat their swords into ploughshares,
>   and their spears into pruning-hooks;
> nation shall not lift up sword against nation,
>   neither shall they learn war any more.   *Isaiah 2.4*

Blessed be God: our hope is in you.

Restore us, O God of hosts;
show the light of your countenance and we shall be saved.

O God of hosts,
how long will you be angered
    despite the prayers of your people?

You have fed them with the bread of tears;
you have given them bowls of tears to drink.

You have made us the derision of our neighbours,
and our enemies laugh us to scorn.

Restore us, O God of hosts;
show the light of your countenance and we shall be saved.

Psalm 80.3–7

In weakness,
in smallness of hope, in vulnerable faith,
we come in penitence
and await your renewing Spirit.   *Dorothy McRae-McMahon*

Surely God is my salvation;
    I will trust, and will not be afraid,
for the Lord God is my strength and my might;
    he has become my salvation.
With joy you will draw water from the wells of salvation.
And you will say on that day:
    Give thanks to the Lord,
        call on his name;
    make known his deeds among the nations;
        proclaim that his name is exalted.   *Isaiah 12.2–4*

Restorer of peace and justice,
we pray for all whose lives are blighted
    by poverty and conflict.
Bless those who make for peace,
sustain those who bind the wounds,
and walk with all who seek your kingdom here on earth.

Peace I leave with you;
my peace I give to you.
I do not give to you as the world gives.
Do not let your hearts be troubled,
and do not let them be afraid.   *John 14.27*

Monday Evening Prayer

When you come to judge the world,
who will not be found wanting?

> For all have sinned and fallen short of the glory of God,
> and God will come in judgement.
> Wake, wake, all hearts, return to the One
> who made all, loves all, calls all,
> and is mightier in graciousness –
> come, our God, and save us!

When you come to judge the world,
who will not be found wanting?

Say among the nations, 'Our God is King!'
God has set the world to rights, so that it will not be shaken;

God will judge the peoples with righteousness.
Let the heavens make merry, and let the earth exult;

let the sea be shaken and everything in it;
let the plains be joyful and all that is in them,
and all the trees of the forest rejoice before God's face;

for God is coming to judge the earth,
and will judge the world in righteousness,
and the peoples with true judgement.   *Psalm 96.10–13 jw*

God our judge, we rejoice in your righteousness
and tremble before your judgement seat.
Awaken our hearts for the coming of your Son,
shake up our will to serve,
that we may greet him with joy
in the work of your kingdom
and find in ourselves
your dwelling place.

Following the way of your judgements, O God, we set our
hope on you; your name and the remembrance of you are the
soul's desire. By night my spirit is awake for you, O God, for
your commandments give light to the world. Learn true justice,
you who dwell on the earth, for the unrighteous have been
silenced. *Isaiah 26.8–9 jw*

O God, all-seeing and compassionate,
stir up the faltering flame of our discipleship,
that we may bring hope to the hopeless,
especially to those who suffer from neglect,
    injustice and oppression
at the hands of their fellow creatures.
We ask this in the name of Jesus Christ,
who came among us to show us the way of true hope.

O mighty Lord, leader of the house of Israel, you appeared to
Moses in the burning bush, and gave him the law on Sinai:
come, and with outstretched arm redeem us. *Traditional*

Tuesday Morning Prayer

Blessed are you, O God: in you we put our trust.

> Those who wait for the Lord shall renew their strength,
>   they shall mount up with wings like eagles,
> they shall run and not be weary,
>   they shall walk and not faint.   *Isaiah 40.31*

Blessed are you, O God: in you we put our trust.

I waited patiently upon you, O God;
you stooped to me and heard my cry.

You lifted me out of the desolate pit,
    out of the mire and the clay;
you set my feet upon a high cliff and made my footing sure.

You put a new song in my mouth,
    a song of praise to our God;
many shall see and stand in awe
    and put their trust in you.

Happy are they who trust in the Most High!
They do not resort to evil spirits or turn to false gods.

Psalm 40.1–4

> In weakness,
> in smallness of hope, in vulnerable faith,
> we come in penitence
> and await your renewing Spirit.   *Dorothy McRae-McMahon*

Be patient, therefore, beloved, until the coming of the Lord. The farmer waits for the precious crop from the earth, being patient with it until it receives the early and the late rains. You also must be patient. Strengthen your hearts, for the coming of the Lord is near. *James 5.7–8*

Tender God, we pray for those
whose waiting is filled with agony:
for all who wait without hope,
who wait alone and lonely,
who wait in the darkness of depression.
Hold them in your motherly arms
and bring them the comfort of your presence.

Now is the time of watching and waiting
a time pregnant with hope
a time to watch and pray. *Kate McIlhagga*

Tuesday Evening Prayer

Our God will surely come, and will not delay.

> You come in storm and disaster,
> you come in quiet and peace,
> you come in what delights us,
> you come in the upsets of life.
> You come in our knowing and our not knowing –
> we wait and watch with hearts and minds
> alert to your loving approach.

Our God will surely come, and will not delay.

On God alone wait in silence, my soul,
for in God is the source of my hope.

God is my God and the one who saves me,
who rescues me so that I shall not be forced to move.

God is my salvation and my glory,
my strong support and my hope.

Place your hopes in God, all my people;
pour out your hearts before God our helper.   *Psalm 62.5–8 jw*

> From our sleepiness of spirit, dear God, set us free,
> from our impatient carelessness, rouse us,
> that we may watch and wait and hope in you,
> and rejoice in all signs of your presence
> in ourselves and in the world around us.

Be alert, be watchful! You do not know when the moment will be upon you. As when householders go away they leave instructions for their servants about each one's task, and the task of the doorkeeper is to stay awake, so you too are to stay awake. You do not know when your master will return, at evening, midnight, cockcrow or dawn. He could suddenly be there and find you asleep. So I tell you again, keep awake!   *Mark 13.33–37 JW*

Dear God,
we pray for those who cannot pray for themselves:
for the very ill,
for those who wait beside them,
for the bereaved,
for those without hope in their lives,
for the impatient,
and for all who are looking for signs of your presence –
may your mercy and love rest upon all your creatures.

O shoot from Jesse's stem, you stand as a sign for the peoples – a sign before whom rulers will fall silent, and whom the Gentiles will seek: come, deliver us, and do not delay!   *Traditional*

Wednesday Morning Prayer

Blessed are you, O God: you hear us when we call.

> The Lord, your God, is in your midst,
>   a warrior who gives victory;
> he will rejoice over you with gladness,
>   he will renew you in his love;
> he will exult over you with loud singing
>   as on a day of festival.
>
> *Zephaniah 3.17*

Blessed are you, O God: you hear us when we call.

Out of the depths have I called to you;
    O God, hear my voice;
let your ears consider well the voice of my supplication.

If you were to note what is done amiss,
O God, who could stand?

For there is forgiveness with you,
therefore you shall be feared.

I wait for you, O God; my soul waits for you;
in your word is my hope.

Psalm 130.1–4

> In weakness,
> in smallness of hope, in vulnerable faith,
> we come in penitence
> and await your renewing Spirit.
>
> *Dorothy McRae-McMahon*

Rejoice in the Lord always; again I will say, Rejoice. Let your gentleness be known to everyone. The Lord is near. Do not worry about anything, but in everything by prayer and supplication with thanksgiving let your requests be made known to God. And the peace of God, which surpasses all understanding, will guard your hearts and your minds in Christ Jesus.

Philippians 4.4–7

Spirit of Truth,
open our minds,
that we may hear your word.
Spirit of Justice,
open our mouths,
that we may be a voice for the voiceless.
Spirit of Compassion,
open our hearts,
that we may share your love in the world.

Prepare the way of the Lord!
The one for whom we wait is near.

Wednesday Evening Prayer

Prepare in the wilderness a highway for our God.

Those whom God has redeemed will return
and they will come to Zion with singing;
everlasting joy will be upon their heads;
for joy and gladness will take hold of them,
and grief, distress and sighing will flee away.   *Isaiah 35.10 JW*

Prepare in the wilderness a highway for our God.

You are our God, your way is perfect,
your words are tested by fire,
you are the shield and defender of all who hope in you.

For who is God except our God?
You gird me with strength, and make my way perfect.

You have made me as fleet-footed as a deer,
and set me in the heights.

You have given me the shield of salvation,
your right hand holds me up
and your training has set me on the path to my goal.

Psalm 18.30–33, 35 JW

When we turn aside from your way, set us right.
When we fail to use your gifts, open our eyes to see.
When we are intent on our own safety and satisfaction,
lead us into the wide spaces of your loving.

This is the witness of John, when the Jews sent priests and
Levites from Jerusalem to ask him, 'Who are you?' And John
confessed – he did not refuse, but confessed, 'I am not the
Christ.' And they asked him, 'So who are you then? Are you
Elijah?' And he answered, 'I am not.' 'Are you the prophet?' And
he answered, 'No'. They said to him, 'Who are you? We need to
give an answer to those who sent us. What do you say about
yourself?' He said: 'I am a voice crying out in the desert, "Make
straight the way of the Lord",' as the prophet Isaiah said.

John 1.19–23 jw

God of the prophets and teachers, we pray:
For those who have lost their way: O God, find them!
For those imprisoned in narrowness: O God, free them!
For those who have given up on the faith they once had:
O God, remind them of yourself and of the power of love!

O Key of David, and ruler of the house of Israel, you open, and
no one can shut, you shut, and no one can open: come, and
bring the prisoners out of captivity, those who sit in darkness
and the shadow of death. *Traditional*

Thursday Morning Prayer

Blessed are you, O God: you come to set your people free.

> By the tender mercy of our God,
> the dawn from on high will break upon us,
> to give light to those who sit in darkness
> and in the shadow of death,
> to guide our feet into the way of peace. *Luke 1.78–79*

Blessed are you, O God: you come to set your people free.

To you, O God, I lift up my soul;
  I put my trust in you;
let me not be humiliated,
  nor let my enemies triumph over me.

Show me your ways, O God,
and teach me your paths.

Lead me in your truth and teach me
for you are the God of my salvation;
  in you have I trusted all the day long. *Psalm 15.1–4*

> In weakness,
> in smallness of hope, in vulnerable faith,
> we come in penitence
> and await your renewing Spirit. *Dorothy McRae-McMahon*

The wilderness and the dry land shall be glad,
    the desert shall rejoice and blossom;
like the crocus it shall blossom abundantly,
    and rejoice with joy and singing.
The glory of Lebanon shall be given to it,
    the majesty of Carmel and Sharon.
They shall see the glory of the Lord,
    the majesty of our God.

Strengthen the weak hands,
    and make firm the feeble knees.
Say to those who are of a fearful heart,
    'Be strong, do not fear!
Here is your God.
    He will come with vengeance,
with terrible recompense.
    He will come and save you.'   *Isaiah 35.1–4*

When I am tempted to meanness,
show me your ways, O God,
and teach me your paths.
When I fail to care for your creation,
show me your ways, O God,
and teach me your paths.
When I am too busy to stand and stare,
show me your ways, O God,
and teach me your paths.

He showed me a little thing, the size of a hazelnut in the palm
of my hand, and it was as round as a ball. I looked at it with
the eye of my understanding and thought: What can this be?
                                                    Julian of Norwich

Thursday Evening Prayer

Blessed are you, O God: do not delay to come to your servants.

> You are my God, and I will praise you;
> you are my God, and I will make you known
>   among the nations;
> all people of the earth will bless you, O God.
> Turn again, O Lord, at the last,
> and do not delay to come to your servants.

Blessed are you, O God: do not delay to come to your servants.

From you comes my praise in the great gathering
    of your people,
my prayers I will offer among those who fear you.

The poor will eat their fill and be satisfied,
and the seekers after you will offer their praises;
their hearts will live for ever and ever.

All the farthest reaches of the earth will remember
and turn to you, the Most High,
and all the families of the nations will bow down before you.

Psalm 22.25–27 jw

> In this season of gifts
> let us keep this truth before us:
> all that we have comes from you, our God,
> and from your own gifts

are we givers.
'Look down, great Master of the feast; O shine,
And turn once more our water into wine!'

Last two lines Henry Vaughan

An angel of the Lord appeared to Joseph in a dream and said to him, 'Joseph, son of David, do not be afraid to take Mary as your wife. For that which has been conceived within her is of the Holy Spirit. She will bear a son, and you will call his name Jesus; for this child will save his people from their sins.'

Matthew 1.20b–21 JW

Dear God, as your people prepare to celebrate
the coming of Jesus your Son, son of Mary,
open our hearts wide,
that he once more may appear in the world
in the transformed lives of all who seek you.

O Dayspring, brightness of everlasting light, and Sun of righteousness: come, give light to those who sit in darkness and in the shadow of death.

Traditional

Friday Morning Prayer

Blessed are you, O God: your steadfast love never ceases,
your mercies never come to an end.

> Water will gush in the desert
> and streams in the wastelands,
> the parched land will become a marsh
> and the thirsty land springs of water.   *Isaiah 35.6–7 NJB*

Blessed are you, O God: your steadfast love never ceases,
your mercies never come to an end.

When our God restored the fortunes of Zion,
then were we like those who dream.

Then was our mouth filled with laughter,
and our tongue with shouts of joy.

Then they said among the nations,
'God has done great things for them.'

Our God has done great things for us,
and we are glad indeed.

Restore our fortunes, O God,
like the watercourses of the Negev.

Those who sowed with tears
will reap with songs of joy.

Those who go out weeping, carrying the seed,
will come again with joy, shouldering their sheaves.   *Psalm 126*

In weakness,
in smallness of hope, in vulnerable faith,
we come in penitence
and await your renewing Spirit.   *Dorothy McRae-McMahon*

In the fifteenth year of Tiberius Caesar's reign . . . the word of
God came to John the son of Zechariah, in the desert. He
went through the whole Jordan area proclaiming a baptism
of repentance for the forgiveness of sins, as it is written in the
book of the sayings of Isaiah the prophet:

A voice of one that cries in the desert:
Prepare a way for the Lord,
make his paths straight!
Let every valley be filled in,
every mountain and hill be levelled,
winding ways be straightened
and rough roads made smooth,
and all humanity will see the salvation of God.   *Luke 3.1–6 NJB*

Faithful God,
we thank you for the prophets, then and now.
We pray for all who call us to faith
and demand justice for the oppressed.

See the light for your journey
and believe that the Spirit always
    moves ahead of you.   *Dorothy McRae-McMahon*

Friday Evening Prayer

Blessed are you, O God:
you bring down the powerful and raise up the powerless.

And you, Bethlehem of Ephratha,
you are the least of the clans of Judah,
yet from you will come forth for me
one who will be ruler of Israel,
whose origins lie at the beginnings of time.
He will stand and shepherd his flock
in the strength of our God,
and the glory of the name of the Most High.

Micah 5.1–2, 4 JW

Blessed are you, O God:
you bring down the powerful and raise up the powerless.

Who is like you, our God? You dwell in the heights
and look down from above upon the lowly
in heaven and on earth.

You raise up the poor from the earth,
and lift up the destitute from the dunghill
to seat them with rulers, with the rulers of your people.

You establish the childless woman with a household,
and make her the happy mother of children.   *Psalm 113.5–9 JW*

All-seeing God, we hear your rebuke of the proud,
and hearing, we repent and turn to you, our hope,
to find our transformation in the coming of your Son.

And it came about that when Elizabeth heard Mary's greeting,
the child leaped in her womb, and Elizabeth was filled with the
Holy Spirit and cried out aloud, saying, 'Blessed are you among
women, and blessed the fruit of your womb. And how has this
happened to me that the mother of my Lord should come to
me? For see how the sound of your greeting no sooner reached
my ears than the child in my womb leaped for joy. And blessed
is she who has trusted that there will be a fulfilment of those
things that were told her from the Lord.'   *Luke 1.41–45 JW*

O God of promise,
sure guarantor of the hopes of all who turn to you in faith,
rescuer of the despised and downtrodden,
light to lighten those who do not yet know you,
comfort and strength for the despairing,
life to the dying:
strong arm of love,
reach out to us all in compassion and mercy.

O Ruler for whom the nations long, you are the cornerstone that
joins the two parts into one: come, save humankind, whom you
formed out of dust.   *Traditional*

Saturday Morning Prayer

Blessed are you, O God: you come to us in Love.

'What no eye has seen, nor ear heard,
nor the human heart conceived,
what God has prepared for those who love him' –
these things God has revealed to us through the Spirit;
for the Spirit searches everything,
even the depths of God.   *1 Corinthians 2.9b–10*

Blessed are you, O God: you come to us in Love.

Your love, O God, for ever will I sing;
from age to age my mouth will proclaim your faithfulness.

For I am persuaded that your love is established for ever;
you have set your faithfulness firmly in the heavens.

'I have made a covenant with my chosen one;
I have sworn an oath to David my servant:

"I will establish your line for ever,
and preserve your throne for all generations."'   *Psalm 89.1–4*

In weakness,
in smallness of hope, in vulnerable faith,
we come in penitence
and await your renewing Spirit.   *Dorothy McRae-McMahon*

In the sixth month the angel Gabriel was sent by God to a town in Galilee called Nazareth, to a virgin betrothed to a man named Joseph, of the House of David; and the virgin's name was Mary. He went in and said to her, 'Rejoice, you who enjoy God's favour! The Lord is with you.' She was deeply disturbed by these words and asked herself what this greeting could mean, but the angel said to her, 'Mary, do not be afraid; you have won God's favour. Look! You are to conceive in your womb and bear a son, and you must name him Jesus.'   *Luke 1.26–31 NJB*

Give us, O God, the will and courage
to struggle with what is complicated in our lives.
Do not let us be content with easy solutions,
but challenge us to live with integrity and pursue what
    is true.

The *hidden ways* by which love sends me
Are such as completely rob me of myself.
That great noise, that loud gift
Of soft stillness makes me deaf.   *Hadewijch of Antwerp*

84

Saturday Evening Prayer

Arise, O God, and come to your resting place.

> We wait for your loving-kindness, O God,
> and listen for your Word.
> We long to see your light shining in the world,
> for all humanity to taste your treasures,
> to seek your face and know your presence.

Arise, O God, and come to your resting place.

You, our God, have chosen Zion,
selected her for your own dwelling:

'This shall be my resting place for ever and ever;
here I will dwell, because I have chosen her.

Her bereaved I will bless abundantly,
her poor I will satisfy with bread.

Her priests I will clothe with salvation,
her faithful ones will rejoice greatly.'   *Psalm 132.13–16 JW*

> Awaken our hearts, dear God of mercy,
> enlighten our minds, dear God of wisdom,
> stir up our longings, dear Spirit of life,
> as we await the coming of your promise.

And there were shepherds in those parts living out in the fields, keeping watch over their flocks at night. And an angel of the Lord appeared to them and the glory of the Lord shone round them, and they were greatly afraid. And the angel said to them, 'Do not be afraid, for behold I bring you good news of a great joy that is for everybody.'   *Luke 2.8–10 jw*

We thank you, Holy One,
for those who have heard your voice
and followed you in every age;
we thank you, Wise One,
for all who follow your way unknowingly;
we thank you, Mighty One, because those who serve you
are so many more than they or we can tell.

O Emmanuel, God with us, our King and Lawgiver, the desire of the nations and their saviour: come, and save us, O Lord our God.   *Traditional*

CHRISTMAS

Sunday Morning Prayer

Blessed are you, O God, for you dwell in our midst.

    The people who walked in darkness
        have seen a great light;
    those who lived in a land of deep darkness –
        on them light has shined.   *Isaiah 9.2*

Blessed are you, O God, for you dwell in our midst.

Holy One,
how exalted is your name in all the world!

Out of the mouths of infants and children
your majesty is praised above the heavens.

When I consider your heavens, the work of your fingers,
the moon and the stars you have set in their courses,

what are mortals that you should be mindful of them?
Mere human beings that you should seek them out?

You have made them little lower than the angels;
you adorn them with glory and honour.   *Psalm 8.1–2, 4–6*

Emmanuel, God with us,
let the light of your love
always shine in our hearts.

In the beginning was the Word, and the Word was with God,
and the Word was God. He was in the beginning with God. All
things came into being through him, and without him not one
thing came into being. What has come into being in him was life,
and the life was the light of all people. The light shines in the
darkness, and the darkness did not overcome it.   *John 1.1–5*

Holy One,
where there is war and hatred,
come, dwell with us;
where there is poverty and despair,
come dwell with us;
where there is sickness and fear,
come, dwell with us;
where there is loneliness and longing,
come, dwell with us.

Love came down at Christmas,
Love all lovely, Love divine.   *Christina Rossetti*

Sunday Evening Prayer

God is in the midst of us.

> Jesus is born in Bethlehem,
> earth and heaven rejoice together;
> a great wonder is shown to us –
> earth and heaven are glad;
> our God has blessed the poor in spirit –
> earth and heaven bow down and worship.

God is in the midst of us.

O Most High, you abide with us for ever;
your seat of judgement is made ready.

You will judge the world in righteousness;
and the nations with equity.

You have become a refuge for the poor,
a timely help for those in distress.

Those who know your name
will entrust their hopes to you, O God,
for you do not abandon those who seek for you.

Sing to the Holy One who dwells in Zion;
proclaim God's deeds among the peoples.   *Psalm 9.7–11 jw*

> Weary with our busy-ness, we rest in your serenity –
> mother, father, Child.

Heaven is here in your simplicity –
mother and Babe.
Silently, silently,
God is with us,
Jesus is here.

The shepherds said to each other, 'Let us now go to Bethlehem and let us see this thing that has happened which the Lord has told us about.' And they hurried along and found Mary and Joseph, and the baby lying in the feeding-trough. After seeing them, they made known what had been said to them about this child. And everyone who heard it was full of wonder at what the shepherds told them. But Mary stored up all that had been said, pondering on it in her heart. And the shepherds went back home glorifying and praising God for everything they had heard and seen, just as it had been told them.   *Luke 2.15b–20 jw*

As shepherds hurried to Bethlehem to see,
we too pause to gaze upon the Life that has come
   among us;
as everyone was full of wonder,
we too marvel at your promises fulfilled in our midst;
as Mary took all this to heart,
we too will go on reflecting on what this birth portends.

We see him come, and know him ours,
Who with his sunshine and his showers
Turns all the patient ground to flowers.   *Robert Herrick*

Monday Morning Prayer

Blessed are you, O God: you make the meek to inherit the earth.

You have shown the strength of your arm,
  you have scattered the proud in their conceit.
You have cast down the mighty from their thrones,
  and lifted up the lowly.
You have filled the hungry with good things,
  and sent the rich away empty.   *From Luke 1.51–53*

Blessed are you, O God: you make the meek to inherit the earth.

God is our refuge and strength,
a very present help in trouble;

therefore we will not fear, though the earth be moved,
and though the mountains be toppled
  into the depths of the sea;

though its waters rage and foam,
and though the mountains tremble at its tumult.

The God of hosts is with us;
the God of Jacob is our stronghold.

Come now and look upon the works of the Most High,
the One who has done awesome things on earth.

It is God who makes war to cease in all the world;
who breaks the bow and shatters the spear
  and burns the shields with fire.

'Be still, then, and know that I am God;
I will be exalted among the nations;
   I will be exalted in the earth.'   *Psalm 46.1–4, 9–11*

   Emmanuel, God with us,
   let the light of your love
   always shine in our hearts.

Jesus said, 'You know that the rulers of the Gentiles lord it over them, and their great ones are tyrants over them. It will not be so among you; but whoever wishes to be great among you must be your servant, and whoever wishes to be first among you must be your slave; just as the Son of Man came not to be served but to serve, and to give his life a ransom for many.'

Matthew 20.25–27

   Into the world of refugee and soldier,
   the soles of your feet have touched the ground.
   Into the world of banker and beggar,
   the soles of your feet have touched the ground.
   Into the world of Jew and Arab,
   the soles of your feet have touched the ground.

   Walk with us, saviour of the poor,
   be a light on our way,
   travel beside the weary,
   fill the broken hearted with hope
   and heal the nations,
   that all may walk
   in the light of the glory of God.   *Kate McIlhagga*

Monday Evening Prayer

O magnify the Lord with me; for God's mercy lasts for ever.

Blessed are the poor, for they are free to hear;
those who have nothing left are able to receive;
those who are fast bound – they know what freedom means.
And God alone knows how to answer human need,
for God's mercy lasts for ever.

O magnify the Lord with me; for God's mercy lasts for ever.

We sing you, O God, a new song,
for you have done marvellous things;
your right hand and holy arm have won you the victory.

You have made known your salvation
in the sight of the peoples,
and revealed your righteous judgement.

You remember your mercy towards Jacob,
and your faithfulness towards the house of Israel.

All the ends of the world have seen
your saving power, O God.   *Psalm 98.1–3 JW*

God of love, we acknowledge you;
God of truth, we confess our fallings away;
God of new life, we thank you, praise you, bless you
for love offered, truth accepted, new life given
    and restored.

Jesus came to Nazareth and entering the synagogue on the Sabbath he stood up to read. He was given the scroll of the prophet Isaiah, and unfolded it to the passage where it is written: 'The spirit of the Lord is upon me and so anointed me to bring good news to the poor; he has sent me to proclaim release to the captives, sight to the blind, freedom to the shattered, and to proclaim the acceptable year of the Lord.' And rolling up the scroll and giving it back to the attendant he sat down. And the eyes of everybody in the synagogue were upon him. Then he began: 'Today this scripture is fulfilled for your ears to hear.'
Luke 4.16–21 JW

Blessed are you,
the God and Father of our Lord Jesus Christ,
Father of mercies and God of all consolation;
you console us in all our afflictions,
so that we in turn can console others who are afflicted,
with the same consolation we ourselves received.
2 Corinthians 1.3–4 JW

Son of God, Jesus Christ, you are not 'Yes' and 'No',
but with you it is always 'Yes'.
For all the promises of God find their 'Yes' in you,
and through you we say 'Amen' to the glory of God.
Based on 2 Corinthians 1.19–20

Tuesday Morning Prayer

————•◆•————

Blessed are you, O God: you love us with a mother's love.

Before I formed you in the womb
   I knew you,
and before you were born
   I consecrated you.   *Jeremiah 1.5a*

Blessed are you, O God: you love us with a mother's love.

You yourself created my inmost parts;
you knit me together in my mother's womb.

I will thank you because I am marvellously made;
your works are wonderful and I know it well.

My body was not hidden from you,
while I was being made in secret
   and woven in the depths of the earth.

Your eyes beheld my limbs, yet unfinished in the womb;
   all of them were written in your book;
they were fashioned day by day,
   when as yet there was none of them.

How deep I find your thoughts, O God!
How great is the sum of them!   *Psalm 139.12–16*

Emmanuel, God with us,
let the light of your love
always shine in our hearts.

In those days a decree went out from Emperor Augustus that all the world should be registered. This was the first registration and was taken while Quirinius was governor of Syria. All went to their own towns to be registered. Joseph also went from the town of Nazareth in Galilee to Judea, to the city of David called Bethlehem, because he was descended from the house and family of David. He went to be registered with Mary, to whom he was engaged and who was expecting a child. While they were there, the time came for her to deliver her child. And she gave birth to her firstborn son and wrapped him in bands of cloth, and laid him in a manger, because there was no place for them in the inn.   *Luke 2.1–7*

Creator God,
in places of war and national suffering,
be born in us today.
Where greed and ambition threaten to destroy
    our communities,
be born in us today.
Where children are abused and suffer neglect,
be born in us today.

Great little one, whose all-embracing birth
Lifts earth to heaven, stoops heaven to earth.

                                              Richard Crashaw

Tuesday Evening Prayer

Blessed be the Word made flesh, and born of Mary.

When the fullness of time had come, O God,
you sent your Son, born of a woman,
born under the law,
to redeem those who were under the law,
so that we might receive adoption
as your children.   *Galatians 4.4–5 jw*

Blessed be the Word made flesh, and born of Mary.

You are my strong support, O God, and my hope from my
    youth;
by you I have been carried from the womb;

since my mother gave birth to me you have been my shelter,
and to you I sing my song of praise for ever.

I have been as it were a marvel to many,
and you are my strong helper.

Let my mouth be filled with your praise
so that I sing of your glory,
and of your splendour all day long.   *Psalm 71.5–8 jw*

Lord Jesus Christ,
our hearts are narrow: open them wide;
our minds are lazy: stir them up;

our lives are little: grow them up in your service,
that in you we may find the true splendour of our
    human nature.

And the Word became flesh and dwelt in our midst; and we
looked upon his glory, the glory of the Father's only Son, full
of grace and truth. And from his fullness we have all received
grace upon grace; whereas the law was given through Moses,
grace and truth came through Jesus Christ. No one has ever
seen God: God's Son, whose being was in the Father's bosom,
he it is who has made God known.   *John 1.14, 16–18 JW*

Jesus our brother, in your coming
God's dwelling place is among humankind.
May all of us your disciples
answer your call to search out and cherish
that which is of God in every human being,
that God may be honoured in love and service
always and everywhere.

Enrich my heart, mouth, hands in me,
with faith, with hope, with charity;
that I may run, rise, rest with thee.   *George Herbert*

Wednesday Morning Prayer

Blessed are you, O God: all creation belongs to you.

My singing heart, my days' doxology, my gold,
I bring for celebration.
My stillness, my glimpses of serenity, my frankincense,
I bring for meditation.
My brokenness, my tears of rage and sorrow, my myrrh,
I bring for sacrifice.   *Kate Compston*

Blessed are you, O God: all creation belongs to you.

God is Sovereign; let the earth rejoice;
let the multitude of the isles be glad.

Clouds and darkness are round about you,
righteousness and justice
    are the foundations of your throne.

The mountains melt like wax at your presence,
at the presence of the Sovereign of the whole earth.

The heavens declare your righteousness,
and all the peoples see your glory.

Light has sprung up for the righteous,
and joyful gladness for those who are true-hearted.

Rejoice in God, you righteous,
and give thanks to God's holy name.   *Psalm 97.1–2, 5–6, 11–12*

Emmanuel, God with us,
let the light of your love
always shine in our hearts.

Arise, shine; for your light has come,
  and the glory of the Lord has risen upon you.
For darkness shall cover the earth,
  and thick darkness the peoples;
but the Lord will arise upon you,
  and his glory will appear over you.
Nations shall come to your light,
  and kings to the brightness of your dawn.

Lift up your eyes and look around;
  they all gather together, they come to you;
your sons shall come from far away,
  and your daughters shall be carried on their nurses' arms.
Then you shall see and be radiant;
  your heart shall thrill and rejoice,
because the abundance of the sea shall be brought to you,
  the wealth of the nations shall come to you.   *Isaiah 60.1–5*

Light of the world,
we thank you for those who are not like us;
we thank you for difference, for the rainbow of nations
  and peoples.
Help us to see you in one another,
and to appreciate the variety of gifts we have to offer.

What else can today's new star cry out from the heavens except:
Arise and be enlightened!   *Aelred of Rievaulx*

Wednesday Evening Prayer

Blessed are you, our God: you have shown yourself in Jesus.

That which was from the beginning,
which we have heard,
which we have seen with our own eyes,
which we have looked upon, and our hands have touched –
his living Word –
this life was manifested to us.
We have seen it and borne witness.   *1 John 1.1, 2a* jw

Blessed are you, our God: you have shown yourself in Jesus.

Let the king judge your people rightly, your poor with justice.
Let the mountains and the hills yield peace for your people.

Let his reign endure and his descendants last as long as the
    sun and moon.
Let him be like the rain falling on mown grass,
like a rain shower soaking the earth.

Let righteousness rise up in his days,
and abundance of peace as long as the moon endures.

Let him rule from sea to sea,
from the river to the ends of the earth.   *Psalm 72.2–8* jw

For all in our doing and thinking that is afraid to come
    to the light,
rebuke us, forgive us, show us your way.

For our meanness and small-mindedness,
rebuke us, forgive us, show us your way.
For our part in obscuring for others the way of Jesus,
rebuke us, forgive us, show us your way.

Then Jesus came from Galilee to the river Jordan to John, to
be baptized by him. John tried to prevent him, saying, 'I should
be baptized by you, and are you coming to me?' In answer Jesus
said to him, 'Let it be, for now – for it is fitting for us to fulfil
all righteousness in this way.' So John agreed. Jesus was baptized
and even as he came up from the water the heavens were laid
open for him, and he saw the Spirit of God coming down like
a dove upon him. And there was a voice from heaven saying,
'This is my beloved Son, in whom I am well pleased.'

Matthew 3.13–17 jw

O Light of the minds that know you,
and Joy of the hearts that love you,
shine forth upon your whole creation;
and especially in your human creatures
burn away dross,
and refine them in your fiery love,
that we may come to share in the truly human desires
embodied in Jesus our Brother,
and be part of the making and remaking
of your reign upon earth.

The glory of God is a living human being,
and to see God is the essence of human life.   *St Irenaeus*

Thursday Morning Prayer

Blessed are you, O God: born of a woman, you took our flesh.

> Do not fear, for I have redeemed you;
> I have called you by name, you are mine.   *Isaiah 43.1*

Blessed are you, O God: born of a woman, you took our flesh.

Come, let us sing to God Most High;
let us shout for joy to the rock of our salvation.

Let us come before God's presence with thanksgiving
and raise a loud shout with psalms.

For you, O God, are a great God,
high above all gods.

In your hand are the depths of the earth,
and the heights of the hills are yours also.

The sea is yours, for you made it,
and your hands have moulded the dry land.

Come, let us bow down and bend the knee,
and kneel before our Maker.   *Psalm 95.1–6*

> Emmanuel, God with us,
> let the light of your love
> always shine in our hearts.

The people who walked in darkness
  have seen a great light;
those who lived in a land of deep darkness –
  on them light has shined.
For a child has been born for us,
  a son given to us;
authority rests upon his shoulders;
  and he is named
Wonderful Counsellor, Mighty God,
  Everlasting Father, Prince of Peace.   *Isaiah 9.2b, 6*

Everyday God,
help us to discover your good news
amid the ordinariness of life.
May we see you in one another
and serve you in serving our neighbour.

Has not God chosen the poor in the world to be rich in faith
and to be heirs of the kingdom that he has promised to those
who love him?   *James 2.5*

Thursday Evening Prayer

Arise, shine, for your light is come!

> God all-bounteous, all-creative,
> whom no ills from good dissuade,
> is incarnate, and a native
> of the very world he made.   *Christopher Smart*

Arise, shine, for your light is come!

O God, my heart is not lifted up,
nor do my eyes look to the heights;

I do not busy myself with great matters,
nor with marvels that are above me,
lest I be brought down.

But I lift up my soul
like a weaned child with its mother,
until you answer me again.   *Psalm 131.1–2 JW*

> Our eyes look to you, Lord Jesus: may we look
> not childishly but simply,
> not nagging, but never failing to ask,
> not complacently, but with fear and trembling
> yet with confidence,
> as one approaches a dearest friend.

And I myself when I was born began to breathe the common air, and fell down upon the earth whose nature I shared, and the first sound I made was to cry, like everyone else. I was wrapped in swaddling clothes and cared for. No king ever had a different kind of beginning. There is one way to come into life for all, and one way to leave it. *Wisdom 7.3–6 JW*

Loving God,
let the learned and the simple praise you together,
for far above us though you are,
you make your home with the humble-hearted;
they stumble and you raise them up;
none fall, who lift up their eyes to you. *St Augustine of Hippo*

The journey to God is the journey into reality.
Barbara Reynolds

Friday Morning Prayer

Blessed are you, O God: glimpsed in a baby.

> Joyful is the dark,
> holy, hidden God,
> rolling cloud of night beyond all naming,
> Majesty in darkness,
> Energy of love,
> Word-in-Flesh, the mystery proclaiming.   *Brian Wren*

Blessed are you, O God: glimpsed in a baby.

The heavens declare the glory of God,
and the firmament shows God's handiwork.

One day tells its tale to another,
and one night imparts knowledge to another.

Although they have no words or language,
and their voices are not heard,

their sound has gone out into all lands,
and their message to the ends of the world.   *Psalm 19.1–4*

> Emmanuel, God with us,
> let the light of your love
> always shine in our hearts.

A shoot shall come out from the stock of Jesse,
    and a branch shall grow out of his roots.
The spirit of the Lord shall rest on him,
    the spirit of wisdom and understanding,
    the spirit of counsel and might,
    the spirit of knowledge and the fear of the Lord.
The wolf shall live with the lamb,
    the leopard shall lie down with the kid,
the calf and the lion and the fatling together,
    and a little child shall lead them.   *Isaiah 11.1–2, 6*

God of Many Names,
in our desire to know you,
let us not confine you;
in our longing to touch you,
may we not cling to you.
Keep us from thinking we understand too much,
and help us to enjoy the mystery of not-knowing.

When peaceful silence lay over all,
and night had run the half of her swift course,
down from the heavens, from the royal throne,
leapt your all-powerful Word.   *Wisdom 18.14–15 NJB*

Friday Evening Prayer

O marvellous exchange! You who came to be with us
are now at work to draw us to yourself.

Today Christ is born,
today a Saviour has appeared;
today on earth angels are singing,
today they cry out and say,
Glory to God in the highest, Alleluia!

Based on an ancient antiphon

O marvellous exchange! You who came to be with us
are now at work to draw us to yourself.

I will exalt you, O God my king,
and bless your name for ever and ever;
every day I will bless you, and praise your name.

How great you are, and greatly to be praised!
Your greatness is immeasurable.

You are compassionate and merciful,
long-suffering and steadfast in love.

You are good to those who wait for you,
and your mercies are over all your works.   *Psalm 145.1–2, 8–9 JW*

Let all creation fall silent before you,
God with us, Child of Mary.
Let our silence be of awe, of love, of wonder,
Emmanuel, God with us.
Let our silence be of joy,
like the great joy of the Magi
when they saw you,
Child of Mary, desire of the nations.
Amen! So be it!

They went on their way and, behold, the star, which they had
seen in the east, went ahead of them, until it came and stood
above where the child was. When they saw the star they were
filled with an overwhelming joy. And coming into the house
they saw the infant child with Mary his mother, and falling on
their knees they worshipped him; and opening their treasure
chest they offered him gifts, gold and frankincense and myrrh.

Matthew 2.9–11 JW

Peace Child,
   in the sleep of the night
   in the dark before light
   you come,
   in the silence of stars
   in the violence of wars –
Savior, your name.

Peace Child,
   to our dark and our sleep
   to the conflict we reap
   now come –
   be your dream born alive,
   held in hope, wrapped in love:
God's true shalom.

Shirley Erena Murray

Saturday Morning Prayer

Blessed are you, O God: you call us to follow a star.

When you pass through the waters, I will be with you;
    and through the rivers, they shall not overwhelm you;
when you walk through fire you shall not be burned,
    and the flame shall not consume you.   *Isaiah 43.2*

Blessed are you, O God: you call us to follow a star.

O God, you have been our refuge
from one generation to another.

Before the mountains were brought forth,
    or the land and the earth were born,
from age to age you are God.

You turn us back to the dust and say,
'Go back, O child of earth.'

For a thousand years in your sight
    are like yesterday when it is past
and like a watch in the night.

Show your servants your works
and your splendour to their children.

May the graciousness of our God be upon us;
prosper the work of our hands;
    prosper our handiwork.   *Psalm 90.1–4, 16–17*

Emmanuel, God with us,
let the light of your love
always shine in our hearts.

The disciples came to Jesus and asked, 'Who is the greatest in the kingdom of heaven?' He called a child, whom he put among them, and said, 'Truly I tell you, unless you change and become like children, you will never enter the kingdom of heaven. Whoever becomes humble like this child is the greatest in the kingdom of heaven. Whoever welcomes one such child in my name welcomes me.   *Matthew 18.1–5*

Baptising Spirit, forgiving and healing,
may we stop and listen
for the sound of angel voices,
stop and search for a star
to lead us to the living Word,
that we might be warmed
by his love.   *Kate McIlhagga*

May the Lord bless us and watch over us,
the Lord make his face shine upon us
    and be gracious to us,
the Lord look kindly on us
    and give us peace.   *Based on Numbers 6.24–26*

Saturday Evening Prayer

Blessed are you, O God, the strength of my life and my joy.

> You are the everlasting One, Creator of the ends of the earth.
> You will not grow faint or weary,
> and your understanding is unsearchable.
> You revive the faint and strengthen the weary.
> Even the youthful can become faint and weary,
> even athletes can stumble;
> but those who wait upon you will renew their strength.
> They will fly on eagles' wings,
> they will run and not be weary,
> they will walk and not faint.   *Isaiah 40.28b–31 JW*

Blessed are you, O God, the strength of my life and my joy.

You are my light and my salvation – whom shall I fear?
You are the shield of my life, from whom shall I shrink?

When those who would harm me come near
  to devour my flesh,
then they themselves, my enemies and oppressors,
  grow weak and fall back.

If I am faced with a hostile crowd, my heart will not be afraid;
if an enemy rises up against me I will not be the one to
  lose hope.

One thing I have asked from you, and this I will earnestly seek,
that I may dwell in your house all the days of my life,
to look upon your beauty, and to visit your temple.

Psalm 27.1–4 JW

Dear God, in your service we pray:
for the courage to take risks,
for attentiveness in moments of decision,
for endurance in times of hardship,
and for joy at the goal set before us.

Truly indeed I tell you that you will weep and mourn, while the world rejoices; you will be distressed, but your sorrow will be turned into joy. A woman in labour is distressed, because her time has come; but when the child is born, she no longer remembers her distress because of her joy that another human being has been born into the world. And you yourselves are now in distress; but I will see you again and your heart will rejoice, and your joy no one will take from you.

John 16.20–22 JW

Loving God,
as the coming of Jesus brought both joy and pain
    into the world,
may all who have put their trust in you in the name of Jesus
find grace and courage to stand before the world
as a community in whom you are still at work,
bringing all creation to fullness of life and joy
in your Son.

And may your blessing remain on all your creation for ever.

LENT

Sunday Morning Prayer

Blessed are you, O God: you sustain us in desert places.

> I will make with them a covenant of peace
> and banish wild animals from the land,
> so that they may live in the wild
> and sleep in the woods securely.   *Ezekiel 34.25*

Blessed are you, O God: you sustain us in desert places.

Turn, O God, and deliver me;
save me for your mercy's sake.

For in death no one remembers you;
and who will give you thanks in the grave?

I grow weary because of my groaning;
every night I drench my bed
    and flood my couch with tears.

My eyes are wasted with grief
and worn away because of all my enemies.

Depart from me, all evildoers,
for God has heard the sound of my weeping.

You, O God, have heard my supplication;
you accept my prayer.   *Psalm 6.4–9*

Remember, O God,
your compassion and love,
for they are from everlasting.

In those days Jesus came from Nazareth of Galilee and was baptized by John in the Jordan. And just as he was coming up out of the water, he saw the heavens torn apart and the Spirit descending like a dove on him. And a voice came from heaven, 'You are my Son, the Beloved; with you I am well pleased.'

And the Spirit immediately drove him out into the wilderness for forty days, tempted by Satan; and he was with the wild beasts; and the angels waited on him.   *Mark 1.9–13*

Living God,
protect all who find themselves in hard times:
those who face an unknown future,
those tempted to abandon hope,
all who struggle with loss of faith.

God did not say, 'You will not be tempted; you will not be sorely troubled; you will not be distressed.' But God said, 'You will not be overcome.'   *Julian of Norwich*

Sunday Evening Prayer

How great your love for us, O God!

> Jesus, driven into the wilderness by God's Spirit,
> Jesus, tired and tempted, watched over by angels,
> Jesus, teaching, healing, arguing, praying,
> Jesus, calling Lazarus out of the tomb,
> Jesus, riding into Jerusalem on an ass,
> Jesus, be with us as we recall once more
> your passion, your dying, your rising again.

How great your love for us, O God!

Behold, O God, your eyes are upon those who fear you,
those who put their hope in your mercy,

to deliver their souls from death,
and to feed them in the time of famine.

Our souls wait upon you,
for you are our help and our strong defender.

In you our hearts find happiness,
and in your holy name we place our hope.

May your mercy, O Holy One, be upon us,
as we have placed our hope in you.   *Psalm 33.18–22 jw*

Holy God, holy and strong, holy and undying,
have mercy upon us.
Be our guide and champion
as we seek renewal of our lives in you.

We urge you not to allow the grace of God you have received
to go to waste; for it says: 'In a favourable time I called to you,
and in the day of salvation I came to your help.' Look, now is
the acceptable time, see, now is the day of salvation! We are
giving no one cause for offence in anything that might fault
our service to God and yourselves, but in every way possible
we are conducting ourselves as God's ministers.

2 Corinthians 6.1–4 jw

Jesus, let us follow you, the master and leader of us all,
on this road that leads, on our own journey to Easter,
to the rediscovery and renewal of your gift to us in baptism.
Glory be to you, who have opened this way for us all!

Hope holds to Christ the mind's own mirror out
to take his lovely likeness more and more.

Gerard Manley Hopkins

Monday Morning Prayer

Blessed are you, O God: you call us to follow the way of Jesus.

> Let us humble ourselves;
> let us strive to know our God,
> whose justice dawns like the morning star;
> its dawning is as sure as the sunrise.   *Hosea 6.3 ssf*

Blessed are you, O God: you call us to follow the way of Jesus.

To you, O God, I lift up my soul;
  in you I put my trust;
let me not be humiliated,
  nor let my enemies triumph over me.

Let none who look to you be put to shame;
let the treacherous be disappointed in their schemes.

Show me your ways, O God,
and teach me your paths.   *Psalm 25.1–3*

> Remember, O God,
> your compassion and love,
> for they are from everlasting.

Jesus called the crowd with his disciples, and said to them, 'If any want to become my followers, let them deny themselves and take up their cross and follow me. For those who want to save their life will lose it, and those who lose their life for my sake, and for the sake of the gospel, will save it. For what will it profit them to gain the whole world and forfeit their life?

Mark 8.34–36

For all who inspire us with their courage,
thanks be to God.
For leaders not afraid to try something new,
thanks be to God.
For prophets who challenge us to be more adventurous,
thanks be to God.
For the chance to share in the building of the kingdom
    here on earth,
thanks be to God.

Be thou a bright flame before me,
Be thou a guiding star above me,
Be thou a smooth path below me ...
Today – tonight – and for ever.   *Carmina Gadelica*

Monday Evening Prayer

Jesus, teacher, companion and guide, go with us on the way.

> You do see, O God: you take notice of trouble and grief,
> and take them into your own hands,
> so the poor take refuge with you,
> and you care for the orphans and widows.
> You hear the crying of the helpless,
> and respond to those in despair.

Jesus, teacher, companion and guide, go with us on the way.

O God, lead me in your righteousness
  in the face of my enemies;
make my way straight before you.

And let all those who put their trust in you
  find happiness with you.
They will rejoice for ever,
  and you will make your home with them.

All those who love your name will make their boast in you,
for you bless the righteous,
surrounding them with the armour of your good pleasure.

Psalm 5.8, 11–12 jw

> When we are weak, remind us of your gracious love;
> when we wander from right paths, direct our footsteps
>   back to you;
> when we feel alone and unprotected, be with us on our way.

And they came into Jericho. And when Jesus was on the way out of Jericho, along with the disciples and a considerable crowd, Bartimaeus the son of Timaeus, a blind beggar, was sitting by the roadside. And hearing that it was Jesus of Nazareth, he started to shout out, 'Jesus, son of David, have pity on me!' And many rebuked him and told him to be quiet. But he shouted out all the more, 'Son of David, have pity on me!' And Jesus stood still and said, 'Call him.' And they called the blind man, saying to him, 'Cheer up, come on, he is calling you.' At that he leapt up, casting aside his outer garment, and came to Jesus. And Jesus responded to him, asking him, 'What do you want me to do?' The blind man replied, 'Teacher, I want to see again.' And Jesus said to him, 'On with you, your faith has saved you.' And he regained his sight and followed him on the way.

Mark 10.46–52 jw

Jesus, stir us up to follow you without looking back,
for the kingdom is God's.
Teach us to be an encouragement,
    and not a stumbling block
to all who seek after you,
for the power is God's.
Let us thank you always for your endlessly generous
    response,
for the glory also is God's, without end.

Though we may absent ourselves, our home does not perish, for it is in your eternity. *St Augustine of Hippo*

Tuesday Morning Prayer

Blessed be God, Provider and Sustainer.

I am about to do a new thing;
    now it springs forth, do you not perceive it?
I will make a way in the wilderness
    and rivers in the desert.

Isaiah 43.19

Blessed be God, Provider and Sustainer.

Remember, O God, your compassion and love,
for they are from everlasting.

Remember not the sins of my youth and my transgressions;
remember me according to your love
    and for the sake of your goodness.

You guide the humble in doing right
and teach your way to the lowly.

Psalm 25.5–6, 8

Remember, O God,
your compassion and love,
for they are from everlasting.

What woman having ten silver coins, if she loses one of them, does not light a lamp, sweep the house, and search carefully until she finds it? When she has found it, she calls together her friends and neighbours, saying, 'Rejoice with me, for I have found the coin that I had lost.' Just so, I tell you, there is joy in the presence of the angels of God over one sinner who repents.

Luke 15.8–10

Gracious God,
be with us as we make preparation
– in our homes, in our lives, in our hearts.
May we never give up our search for you
nor our desire to be found by you.

I would like the angels of heaven to be among us.
I would like the abundance of peace.
I would like full vessels of charity.
I would like rich treasures of mercy.
I would like cheerfulness to preside over all.
I would like Jesus to be present.　　　*Attributed to St Brigid*

Tuesday Evening Prayer

Blessed are you, O God: you keep renewing the earth.

> Blessed Creator, Father and Mother of all that is made,
> Fashioner of planet Earth,
> where Lent is springtime, seed-time, new life emerging,
> old life renewed;
> and also harvest-time, season of richness, fruitfulness,
> all life fulfilled.
> In both is labour, pain and death,
> and also life abundant.
> Praise be to you!

Blessed are you, O God: you keep renewing the earth.

A clean heart create in me, O God,
and renew an upright spirit in my inmost parts.

Do not cast me away out of your sight,
or take away your Holy Spirit from me.

Give me back the joy of your salvation,
and strengthen me with your guiding Spirit.

An offering fit for God is a humbled spirit;
a heart that is humble and contrite God will not despise.

Psalm 51.10–12, 17 jw

Show us your ways, Holy One, and we see that we fall short;
lead us on your path, and we dare to leave our baggage
    behind;
point us to our goal, and raise us to new life in you.

Who then is the faithful and shrewd servant whom his master
put in charge of his household to give them their food at the
appropriate time? Blessed is that servant whom the master when
he comes will find acting in this way. Truly I tell you, he will
set him over all his possessions. But if that bad servant says to
himself, 'My master is taking a long time', and begins to strike
his fellow servants, and eats and drinks with the drunkards, the
master of that servant will come on a day he does not expect
him, and at an hour he does not know, and the master will cut
him off and place him with the hypocrites, where there will be
weeping and gnashing of teeth.   *Matthew 24.45–51 jw*

O God, our God, it is said that you are a consuming fire;
and that you are also infinite love and mercy:
in this world of terrible hatreds, conflict and ill-will,
grant that we may not regard any others, or ourselves,
as beyond the reach of your unconquerable love.

O God, keep our faces turned towards you,
that some day others may see your face in us.

Wednesday Morning Prayer

Blessed are you, O God: you made us to care for the earth.

> The earth is God's and all that is in it,
> the world and all who dwell therein.
> For it is God who founded it upon the sea
> and made it firm upon the rivers of the deep. *Psalm 24.1–2*

Blessed are you, O God: you made us to care for the earth.

My soul cleaves to the dust;
give me life according to your word.

I have confessed my ways and you answered me;
instruct me in your statutes.

Make me understand the way of your commandments
that I may meditate on your marvellous works.

I will run the way of your commandments,
for you have set my heart at liberty. *Psalm 119.25–27, 32*

> Remember, O God,
> your compassion and love,
> for they are from everlasting.

Is not this the fast that I choose:
   to loose the bonds of injustice,
   to undo the thongs of the yoke,
to let the oppressed go free,
   and to break every yoke?
Is it not to share your bread with the hungry,
   and bring the homeless poor into your house;
when you see the naked, to cover them,
   and not to hide yourself from your own kin?
Then your light shall break forth like the dawn,
   and your healing shall spring up quickly.   *Isaiah 58.6–8a*

Creator God,
give us the will to share the fruits of your creation,
that no one may go hungry or homeless or naked.
Give us minds to understand the connectedness of all
   living things,
hearts that yearn for your kingdom,
and hands ready to loose the bonds of injustice.

I gird myself today with the might of heaven:
The rays of the sun,
The beams of the moon,
The glory of fire,
The speed of wind,
The depth of the sea,
The stability of earth,
The hardness of rock.   *Anon.*

Wednesday Evening Prayer

You look upon all that you have made, O God,
and behold, it is very good!

Praise to you, Maker of makers,
for the marvellous diversity of living beings,
for the wonders and mystery of the universe,
for the exploring minds of your human creatures,
for hearts to love and serve each other,
and to respect and cherish all created things.
To you be the glory for ever!

You look upon all that you have made, O God,
and behold, it is very good!

'Listen, my people, and I will speak to you,
Israel, I will solemnly bear witness against you –
I am God, your God.

I will not reprove you for your sacrifices –
your burnt offerings are always before me;

I do not want calves from your homestead,
or he-goats from your folds.

For all the animals of the woodlands are mine,
and the flocks and herds on the mountainsides.

I know all the flying creatures of the heavens
and the fruits of the fields are mine too.

If I were hungry, I certainly would not tell you,
for mine is the earth and everything on it.'

Make your offering to God one of praise,
and let your prayers be what you owe to the Most High.

Psalm 50.7–8, 10–14 JW

Open our hearts to be truly compassionate,
clear our minds to know what we need to do,
inspire our spirits to search for and act on the truth.

Do not strive after death, mistaking it for life, and do not bring
on destruction through the works of your hands. For God did not
make death, nor does he delight in the destruction of the living.
For he created everything so that it could exist, and the continu-
ing generation of living beings in the world is approved by
him – there is no destructive poison there, death does not reign
on earth. For righteousness is immortal.   *Wisdom 1.12–15* JW

Provident God,
lead all peoples to respect your created world;
make us grateful for plenty, eager to share,
restrained in claiming for ourselves,
and inventive in working with others
for the good of all.

You are the hope of all the ends of the earth
and of the remotest seas.

Thursday Morning Prayer

Blessed are you, O God: you stoop to wash our feet.

Many waters cannot quench love,
neither can floods drown it.
If one offered for love all the wealth of one's house
it would be utterly scorned.   *Song of Solomon 8.7*

Blessed are you, O God: you stoop to wash our feet.

I love you, O God,
because you have heard the voice of my supplication,
because you have inclined your ear to me
whenever I called upon you.

The cords of death entangled me;
the grip of the grave took hold of me;
I came to grief and sorrow.

Then I called upon your name:
'O God, I pray you, save my life.'

Gracious are you, O God, and righteous;
you are full of compassion.

You watch over the innocent;
I was brought very low and you helped me.

Turn again to your rest, O my soul,
for God has treated you well.   *Psalm 116.1–6*

Remember, O God,
your compassion and love,
for they are from everlasting.

The Lord spoke to Moses and said, 'I have heard the complaining of the Israelites; say to them, "At twilight you shall eat meat, and in the morning you shall have your fill of bread; then you shall know that I am the Lord your God."'

In the evening quails came up and covered the camp; and in the morning there was a layer of dew around the camp. When the layer of dew lifted, there on the surface of the wilderness was a fine flaky substance, as fine as frost on the ground. When the Israelites saw it, they said to one another, 'What is it?' For they did not know what it was. Moses said to them, 'It is the bread that the Lord has given you to eat.' *Exodus 16.11–15*

Loving God,
we thank you for calling us into community;
may we learn to share ourselves and all that we have.
In remembering the actions of Jesus,
may we learn what it means to serve one another.

Even if it could come about unexpectedly that I live as a recluse in a tiny hut, with the ocean waves surrounding me on all sides, cutting me off from the sight and knowledge of all creatures, not even so do I think I would be free of the snares of this frail world, but there too I am afraid that somehow the love of money could succeed in carrying me off. *Cuthbert of Lindisfarne*

Thursday Evening Prayer

Praise be to you, Giver of all that is good!

O the depth of the riches of your wisdom and knowledge!
How unsearchable your judgements!
How untraceable your paths!
For who knows your mind, O God?
Who is your fellow counsellor?
Who has given to you and made you a debtor?
For from you and through you and for you
is everything –
to you be glory for ever and ever!   *Romans 11.33–36 JW*

Praise be to you, Giver of all that is good!

With what shall I repay the Most High,
    who is so generous to me?
I will take the cup of salvation,
and I will call upon the name of our God.

O Holy One, I am your servant,
your servant and the child of your handmaid;
and you have broken the bonds that have bound me.

I will offer to you an offering of praise;
I will fulfil my vows to you before all the people,

in the courts of your house, O God,
in the midst of you, O Jerusalem.   *Psalm 116.12–13, 16–19 JW*

Dear God, give us
gratitude in receiving,
generosity in giving,
discernment in everything,
that your name may be glorified
and our lives transformed in your image.

After Judas had left them Jesus said, 'Now the Son of Man is
glorified, and God is glorified in him, and God will glorify
him in himself, and he will glorify him at once. Little children,
for a little while only I am with you; you will seek me and, as
I said to the Jews, where I am going you cannot come, and
I tell you that now. A new commandment I give you, that you
love one another; just as I have loved you, you too are to love
one another. This is how everyone will know that you are my
disciples, if you have love for each other.'   *John 13.31–35 JW*

Generous Son of God,
feed us with your own life
that we may be co-workers with you,
to rid the world of all meanness of spirit,
envy and greed,
hatred and violence,
and to nurture lives of fruitful compassion,
friendship and humanity
in us all.

You hear the words 'The body of Christ',
and you reply 'Amen'.
Be a member of the body of Christ
so that your Amen may be true.   *St Augustine of Hippo*

Friday Morning Prayer

Blessed are you, O God: you hear our cries of desolation.

I have come into deep waters,
and the torrent washes over me.
I have grown weary with my crying;
    my throat is inflamed;
my eyes have failed from looking for my God.   *Psalm 69.3–4*

Blessed are you, O God: you hear our cries of desolation.

O God, hear my prayer and let my cry come before you;
hide not your face from me in the day of trouble.

Incline your ear to me;
when I call, make haste to answer me,

for my days drift away like smoke,
and my bones are hot as burning coals.

My heart is smitten like grass and withered,
so that I forget to eat my bread.

Because of the voice of my groaning
I am but skin and bones.

I have become like a vulture in the wilderness,
like an owl among the ruins.

My days pass away like a shadow,
and I wither like the grass.

But you, O God, endure for ever,
and your name from age to age. *Psalm 102.1–6, 11–12*

Remember, O God,
your compassion and love,
for they are from everlasting.

When the days drew near for him to be taken up, he set his face
to go to Jerusalem. And he sent messengers ahead of him. On
their way they entered a village of the Samaritans to make ready
for him; but they did not receive him, because his face was set
towards Jerusalem. When his disciples James and John saw it,
they said, 'Lord, do you want us to command fire to come down
from heaven and consume them?' But he turned and rebuked
them. Then they went to another village. *Luke 9.51–56*

Naked God,
you confront us with your powerlessness
as we watch and wait.
Be with us in our grieving,
and in our hoping.

God of Wounded Hands,
Web and Loom of love,
in your glory come and meet us,
Carpenter of new creation. *Brian Wren*

Friday Evening Prayer

We bow before your cross, O Jesus,
and glorify your holy resurrection.

You told your disciples:
Take heart, I have overcome the world.
You sat in darkness and in the shadow of death,
and in those depths your love embraced humankind;
though all the earth shakes at its loss,
afterwards a profound silence falls,
for by your cross you have redeemed the world.

We bow before your cross, O Jesus,
and glorify your holy resurrection.

I have cried out before you, O God, all day long,
and stretched out my hands to you.

Do you work wonders for the dead?
Do the healers rise up and praise you?

Does anyone talk of your mercy in the tomb,
of your faithfulness in the place of destruction?

Is there awareness of your wonders in the darkness,
or of your righteousness in the place of forgetfulness?

But for myself I do cry out to you, my God,
and my prayer to you is made before the morning comes.

Psalm 88.9b–13 JW

Jesus said:
'Forgive them, Father, for they do not understand
   what they are doing.'
He said: 'Woman, here is your son';
   and to his disciple: 'Here is your mother.'
He said: 'Today you will be with me in Paradise.'
He said: 'My God, my God, why have you abandoned me?'
He said: 'I am thirsty.'
He said: 'Into your hands I commit my spirit.'
He said: 'It is accomplished!'

And the Temple curtain was torn in half from top to bottom. But when the centurion, who was standing nearby facing Jesus, saw that he had breathed his last, he said, 'Truly this man was a son of God.'

There were also women looking on from a distance, among them Mary Magdalene and Mary the mother of the younger James and Joses, and Salome. They had all followed him when he was in Galilee, and ministered to him, along with many other women who had gone up with him to Jerusalem.

Mark 15.38–41 jw

God, let old hatreds die, and all that is not of you.
Let us pause at the empty cross of Jesus,
and follow him, as best we may,
into death's silence,
cleaving to the hope for the world that lies with him
in your hands, O God.

The Cross is the abyss of wonder, the centre of desires, the school of virtues, the house of wisdom, the throne of love, the theatre of joys, and the place of sorrows. It is the root of happiness, and the gate of heaven.   *Thomas Traherne*

Saturday Morning Prayer

Blessed are you, O God: you watch with us in our darkness.

> My soul waits for you
>> more than the night-watch for the morning,
> more than the night-watch for the morning. *Psalm 130.5*

Blessed are you, O God: you watch with us in our darkness.

My God, hear my prayer,
    and in your faithfulness heed my supplications;
answer me in your righteousness.

My spirit faints within me;
my heart within me is desolate.

I remember the time past;
    I muse upon all your deeds;
I consider the works of your hands.

I spread out my hands to you;
my soul gasps to you like a thirsty land.

Let me hear of your loving-kindness in the morning,
    for I put my trust in you;
show me the road that I must walk,
    for I lift up my soul to you. *Psalm 143.1, 4–6, 8*

> Remember, O God,
> your compassion and love,
> for they are from everlasting.

When it was evening, there came a rich man from Arimathea, named Joseph, who was also a disciple of Jesus. He went to Pilate and asked for the body of Jesus; then Pilate ordered it to be given to him. So Joseph took the body and wrapped it in a clean linen cloth and laid it in his own new tomb, which he had hewn in the rock. He then rolled a great stone to the door of the tomb and went away. Mary Magdalene and the other Mary were there, sitting opposite the tomb.

Matthew 27.57–61

Faithful God,
be with us in our in-between times.
Comfort all who are confined by the past
and fearful of the future.
Help us to know that you are present with us always.

Christ who has trod the way before,
lift our spirits as we await the dawn.

Saturday Evening Prayer

We wait for your loving-kindness, O God of our hope.

You are good to those who wait for you,
to those who seek you.
It is good to wait quietly for your salvation,
to endure your absence without relief, as far as one can
   bear it,
to wait alone in silence, when that is all there is to do.
For you will not abandon us for ever –
though you leave us in grief, you will have compassion.
You do not willingly afflict your human children.

Adapted from Lamentations 3.25–33 jw

We wait for your loving-kindness, O God of our hope.

It is good to give thanks to you, O God,
and sing praises to your name, Most High;

to tell of your mercy in the morning,
and of your faithfulness when evening comes.

How mighty are your works, O God,
how weighty your judgements.

The person without sense cannot know them,
the ignorant cannot understand these things.

While sinners spring up like grass,
the disobedient are all brought low,
so as to be destroyed eternally,

but you, O God, are the Most High for ever.

Psalm 92.1–2, 5–8 jw

O God, we have fled to you for refuge:
give us, we pray, your strong encouragement
to seize the hope set before us,
the hope that enters into that inner shrine
where Jesus has gone as our forerunner,
and where he always lives to make intercession for us.

Who has gone up into the heavens and taken wisdom and brought
her down out of the clouds? Who has crossed the sea and found
her and will bring her back, paying in pure gold? There is no
one who knows her path, nor anyone who ponders on her way;
but the One who sees all things knows her, searches her out
by understanding. The one who formed the earth for all of
time and filled it with four-footed creatures; the one who sends
forth the light and it goes its way, who summoned it and it
obeyed trembling. The stars shone in their posts and were glad;
he called them and they said, 'Here we are!' They shone with
joy for the one who made them. This is our God, no other
comes near him. *Baruch 3.29–35 jw*

Jesus, new and living way, give your motley flock
confidence to draw near with you to God our Maker;
hold us fast in unwavering hope, as you are faithful;
stir us up to carry out the works of love and compassion
    towards all in need,

that your name may be known and honoured
   in our generation.

So when that day and hour shall come
in which thyself will be the Sun,
thou'lt find me dressed and on my way,
watching the break of that great day.   *Henry Vaughan*

EASTER

Sunday Morning Prayer

Alleluia, blessed be the God of Jesus Christ,
risen from the dead, alleluia.

 Sing for joy, O heavens,
  and exult, O earth;
 break forth, O mountains,
  into singing.   *Isaiah 49.13a*

Alleluia, blessed be the God of Jesus Christ,
risen from the dead, alleluia.

Rejoice in God, you righteous;
it is good for the just to sing praises.

Praise God with the harp;
play to God upon the psaltery and lyre.

Sing for the Holy One a new song;
sound a fanfare with all your skill upon the trumpet.

For your word, O God, is right,
and all your works are sure.

You love righteousness and justice;
your loving-kindness fills the whole earth.   *Psalm 33.1–5*

145

Christ the Daystar,
dawn in our hearts
and dispel the shades of night.

Mary stood weeping outside the tomb. As she wept, she bent
over to look into the tomb; and she saw two angels in white,
sitting where the body of Jesus had been lying, one at the head
and the other at the feet. They said to her, 'Woman, why are you
weeping?' She said to them, 'They have taken away my Lord,
and I do not know where they have laid him.' When she had
said this, she turned round and saw Jesus standing there, but she
did not know that it was Jesus. Jesus said to her, 'Woman, why
are you weeping? For whom are you looking?' Supposing him
to be the gardener, she said to him, 'Sir, if you have carried him
away, tell me where you have laid him, and I will take him away.'
Jesus said to her, 'Mary!' She turned and said to him in Hebrew,
'Rabbouni!' (which means Teacher).   *John 20.11–16*

Risen Friend,
here, now, on this joyous day,
as we run to greet you,
give us courageous hearts
to turn from the comforts of the night that is past
and welcome the dawn of resurrection.

Bless, O Christ, my face,
Let my face bless everything;
Bless, O Christ, mine eye,
Let mine eye bless all it sees.   *Carmina Gadelica*

Sunday Evening Prayer

Alleluia, alleluia, the Lord is risen indeed, alleluia.

> Most wonderful of all mysteries!
> Christ once raised from the dead dies no more;
> no more has death dominion over him.
> Dead to sin once and for all,
> he is alive for ever with you, our God.   *Romans 6.9–10 JW*

Alleluia, alleluia, the Lord is risen indeed, alleluia.

Open for me the gates of righteousness;
I will enter by them to give thanks to you, the Most High.

This is your gate, O Holy One;
the righteous will enter through it.

I will give thanks to you, O God, because you listened to me,
and you have become my salvation.

The stone that the builders rejected,
this very one has become the cornerstone.

This is your doing, O God,
and it is marvellous for us to see.

This is the day that you have made;
this day we celebrate with joy.   *Psalm 118.19–24 JW*

Lord Jesus Christ,
as we were buried with you in baptism,
so in baptism we are raised with you,
because we have faith in God's working
in you and in us.
And if raised with you, we set our minds on you,
for you are our life and our hope.

Jesus stood among them and said to them, 'Peace be with you.' They were startled and became fearful, thinking that they were seeing a ghost. And he said to them, 'Why this dismay? What are all these thoughts running through your hearts? See my hands and my feet – it is I myself. Touch me and see – a ghost does not have flesh and bones as you see that I have.' And saying this he showed them his hands and his feet.

Then he opened their minds to understand the Scripture, telling them, 'This is how it is written, that the Christ would suffer and be raised from the dead on the third day, and that forgiveness in his name should be proclaimed to all the nations, beginning from Jerusalem; and that you yourselves are witnesses of this. And I am sending what my Father promises upon you; but you must remain in the city until you are clothed with power from above.'   *Luke 24.36b–40, 45–49* JW

Gracious God,
as we celebrate with awe and wonder
the dying and rising again of Jesus your Son,
we ask that your church may embody
more vividly and compellingly
your undying love for your creation;
that the troubled, the oppressed, the disillusioned,
the dying and those who mourn
may see, hear and receive

the good news of our human destiny
to glorify and enjoy you for ever.

So enter, everyone, into the joy of our Lord.
For Christ, being raised from the dead,
has become the first fruits of those who have fallen asleep.
To him be glory and dominion now and for ever.

St John Chrysostom

Monday Morning Prayer

Alleluia, blessed be God, bringer of new life, alleluia.

Fountain of the garden,
well of living water,
streams flowing down from Lebanon!   *Song of Songs 4.15 NJB*

Alleluia, blessed be God, bringer of new life, alleluia.

Praise God from the earth,
you sea-monsters and all deeps;

fire and hail, snow and fog,
tempestuous wind, doing God's will;

mountains and all hills,
fruit trees and all cedars;

wild beasts and all cattle,
creeping things and winged birds;

kings of the earth and all peoples,
princes and all rulers of the world;

young men and maidens,
old and young together.

Let them praise your name, O Most High,
for your name only is exalted,
your splendour is over earth and heaven.   *Psalm 148.7–13*

Christ the Daystar,
dawn in our hearts
and dispel the shades of night.

Jesus put before them another parable: 'The kingdom of heaven
is like a mustard seed that someone took and sowed in his field;
it is the smallest of all the seeds, but when it has grown it is the
greatest of shrubs and becomes a tree, so that the birds of the
air come and make their nests in its branches.'

He told them another parable: 'The kingdom of heaven is like
yeast that a woman took and mixed in with three measures of
flour until all of it was leavened.'   *Matthew 13.31–33*

Creator God,
you invite us to join in your creation,
not just as those who receive
but as co-makers with you.
Teach us to cherish our natural world,
to share its rich resources
and delight in its ever-newness.

When I see the new moon,
    It becomes me to lift mine eye,
It becomes me to bend my knee,
    It becomes me to bow my head.   *Carmina Gadelica*

Monday Evening Prayer

Alleluia, sing to our God a new song, alleluia.

A new song, a new gift, a new life –
dear God, we hear the song and rejoice,
we hold out our hands for the gift,
and find it already within us.
We rejoice, and when the celebratory noise dies down,
we rejoice again at the silence of your presence
with us and ahead of us,
not in our grasp, but securely holding us –
a new song, a new gift, a new life.

Alleluia, sing to our God a new song, alleluia.

O God, I will sing a new song to you,
on a ten-stringed harp I will play for you,

who bestowed salvation on kings,
who redeemed David your servant.

You blessed the people with such gifts as these,
and blessed are the people for whom you are God.

Psalm 144.9–10, 15 jw

Dear God, so far beyond our understanding,
but at the very heart of our being,
help us to grow to our full stature in you,
that we may know as we are known
and love as only you can teach us.

If then you have been raised with Christ, seek what is above, where Christ is seated at the right hand of God. Keep your minds on what is above, not on what is on the earth. For you have died and your life is hidden with Christ in God. When Christ appears, he who is your life, then you too will appear with him in glory.

Colossians 3.1–4 JW

In the name of the risen Jesus
who goes ahead of us,
we pray for all seekers after you, O God,
all new believers,
all those whose faith has faded,
and for all Christians,
that our everyday life may, in ways unknown to us,
draw others to you,
O gracious God.

Hail the Lord of earth and heaven,
Praise to thee by both be given;
Thee we greet triumphant now,
Hail, the resurrection thou!

Charles Wesley

Tuesday Morning Prayer

Alleluia, blessed be God: you come to redeem us, alleluia.

> How beautiful upon the mountains
>> are the feet of the messenger who announces peace,
> who brings good news,
>> who announces salvation.   *Isaiah 52.7*

Alleluia, blessed be God: you come to redeem us, alleluia.

I will exalt you, O God,
  because you have lifted me up
and have not let my enemies triumph over me.

My God, I cried out to you,
and you restored me to health.

You brought me up from the dead;
you restored my life as I was going down to the grave.

Sing to our God, you servants of the Most High;
give thanks for the remembrance of God's holiness.

For the wrath of God endures but the twinkling of an eye,
God's favour for a lifetime.

Weeping may spend the night,
but joy comes in the morning.   *Psalm 30.1–6*

Christ the Daystar,
dawn in our hearts
and dispel the shades of night.

Now there was a woman who had been suffering from hae-
morrhages for twelve years; and though she had spent all she
had on physicians, no one could cure her. She came up behind
Jesus and touched the fringe of his clothes, and immediately
her haemorrhage stopped. Then Jesus asked, 'Who touched me?'
When all denied it, Peter said, 'Master, the crowds surround you
and press in on you.' But Jesus said, 'Someone touched me; for
I noticed that power had gone out from me.' When the woman
saw that she could not remain hidden, she came trembling;
and falling down before him, she declared in the presence of
all the people why she had touched him, and how she had been
immediately healed. He said to her, 'Daughter, your faith has
made you well; go in peace.'   *Luke 8.43–48*

Redeeming God,
we pray for all whose lives are marred by pain and sickness,
for those whose illness causes them isolation or shame.
When we cannot or will not reach out to you,
help us to know that you reach out to us.

Set us free,
heal our wounds,
O God who never leaves us
nor forsakes us.   *Dorothy McRae-McMahon*

Tuesday Evening Prayer

Alleluia, let God's people come with gladness, alleluia.

> And there will be a clear way there,
> and it will be called a holy way, and no one unclean will
>   go upon it,
> but God's people who were scattered will pass over it,
> and they will not be led astray.
> God's redeemed and gathered people will return by it,
> and come to Zion with joy,
> and everlasting gladness will crown them.   *Isaiah 35.8, 10a JW*

Alleluia, let God's people come with gladness, alleluia.

You are my strength and my refuge,
and for the sake of your name you guide and sustain me.

You rescue me from this trap that has been laid for me,
because you are my protector.

Into your hands I entrust my life;
you will rescue me, O God in whom I trust.

Let all your holy ones love you,
for you seek out those who trust you,
and repay the exceedingly arrogant.

Let them be of good courage, and of a stout heart,
all those who hope in you, our God.   *Psalm 31.3–5, 23–24 JW*

Easter God, deliver us from fear of joy,
from cynicism and mediocrity,
and let us be surprised by you every day.

Who can separate us from the love of Christ? Can distress or constraints or persecution or famine or nakedness or sword? As it is written, 'On your account we are put to death all day long, we are reckoned as sheep for slaughtering.' But all these things we have more than overcome through him who loved us. For I am quite sure that neither death nor life nor angels nor principalities nor things present nor things to come, nor powerful forces nor height nor depth nor any other created thing will be able to separate us from the love of God that is in Christ Jesus our Lord.   *Romans 8.35–39 JW*

Risen Jesus, restorer of life to those who turn to you,
we pray for all who are held back
by fear, impatience or a need for certainty.
Give us all a firmer sense of joy in our lives,
a readiness to admit we do not have all the answers,
and a willingness to learn from our mistakes.

And let nothing separate you from the love of God that is in you.

Wednesday Morning Prayer

Alleluia, blessed are you, O God,
ever-renewing your creation, alleluia.

> See, today I appoint you over nations
>   and over kingdoms,
> to pluck up and to pull down,
> to destroy and to overthrow,
> to build and to plant.   *Jeremiah 1.10*

Alleluia, blessed are you, O God,
ever-renewing your creation, alleluia.

I have set you, O God, always before me;
because you are at my right hand I shall not fall.

My heart, therefore, is glad and my spirit rejoices;
my body also shall rest in hope.

For you will not abandon me to the grave,
nor let your holy one see the Pit.

You will show me the path of life;
in your presence there is fullness of joy,
and in your right hand are pleasures for evermore.   *Psalm 16.8–11*

> Christ the Daystar,
> dawn in our hearts
> and dispel the shades of night.

Jesus summoned his twelve disciples and gave them authority over unclean spirits, to cast them out, and to cure every disease and every sickness.

These twelve Jesus sent out with the following instructions: 'Go nowhere among the Gentiles, and enter no town of the Samaritans, but go rather to the lost sheep of the house of Israel. As you go, proclaim the good news. "The kingdom of heaven has come near." Cure the sick, raise the dead, and cleanse the lepers, cast out demons. You received without payment; give without payment. Take no gold, or silver, or copper in your belts, no bag for your journey, or two tunics, or sandals, or a staff; for labourers deserve their food.' *Matthew 10.1, 5–10*

Demanding God,
you call us out of our safety-zones
to join with you in creating your world.
As we pray 'your kingdom come',
give us the courage to be faithful to that call.

May the God who shakes heaven and earth,
whom death could not contain,
who lives to disturb and heal us,
bless us with power to go forth
and proclaim the gospel.

Janet Morley

Wednesday Evening Prayer

Alleluia, blessed is Jesus, the true Cornerstone, alleluia.

No longer are we strangers or foreigners,
but fellow citizens with the saints
and members of God's household,
built upon the foundation laid by the apostles and prophets,
the cornerstone being Christ Jesus himself,
in whom the whole building is fitted together
to grow into a holy temple in the Lord,
in whom we too are built to become the dwelling place of God
by God's own Spirit.   *Ephesians 2.19–22 JW*

Alleluia, blessed is Jesus, the true Cornerstone, alleluia.

Blessed are those who fear you, O God,
and willingly keep your commandments.

They make light spring up in darkness for the upright,
they are generous, compassionate and just.

The good are merciful and lend,
and order their words with good judgement.

Thus they will never be shaken in their path;
those who are just and generous will always be remembered.

They will not be afraid of any hostile rumours,
for their heart is constant in its trust in you.   *Psalm 112.1, 4–7 JW*

Risen Jesus, you call us to work with you for God's kingdom:
teach us not to overvalue our own work,
nor to draw back from fear of failure,
but to entrust our thoughts, words and actions to you.

What is Apollos? And what is Paul? Ministers through whom
you came to believe, and as the Lord granted to each. I planted,
Apollos watered, but God made the plants grow. So neither the
planter nor the waterer amounts to anything, but only God who
makes things grow. The one who plants and the one who waters
are in the same category, but each will get their own reward
according to their own labour. We are fellow workers with God,
while God's is the farmland, and God's the household.

1 Corinthians 3.5–9 jw

God of all peoples,
in this world of many faiths and none,
bless all those who try
to draw together people of good will,
to sort out quarrelling and disputes,
to encourage the faint-hearted,
to check the impatient,
to seek out the good in everyone,
and that which will hold together and unite
all that builds your kingdom on earth.

And may the only wise God be with us all.

Thursday Morning Prayer

Alleluia, blessed be God, Bread of Life, alleluia.

God is light,
    in whom there is no darkness at all.
If we walk in the light,
    as God is in the light,
we have fellowship with one another. *from 1 John 1.5–7*

Alleluia, blessed be God, Bread of Life, alleluia.

Give thanks to our God, who is good;
whose mercy endures for ever.

I shall not die, but live,
and declare the works of the Most High.

You have punished me sorely,
but you did not hand me over to death.

'You are my God and I will thank you;
you are my God and I will exalt you.'

Give thanks to our God, who is good;
whose mercy endures for ever. *Psalm 118.1, 17–18, 28–29*

Christ the Daystar,
dawn in our hearts
and dispel the shades of night.

As they came near the village to which they were going, he walked ahead as if he were going on. But they urged him strongly, saying, 'Stay with us, because it is almost evening and the day is now nearly over.' So he went in to stay with them. When he was at the table with them, he took bread, blessed and broke it, and gave it to them. Then their eyes were opened, and they recognized him; and he vanished from their sight. They said to each other, 'Were not our hearts burning within us while he was talking to us on the road, while he was opening the scriptures to us?'

Luke 24.28–32

God who walks with us,
may we recognize you in all whom we meet today:
in our friends and familiar companions,
and in the unknown stranger.
Help us to see that friendship is both gift and task.

'I was hungry and you gave me food,
I was thirsty and you gave me drink,
I was a stranger and you made me welcome.'

Matthew 25.35 NJB

Thursday Evening Prayer

Alleluia, blessed are you who offer us life in abundance,
  alleluia.

  Beloved, if this is how God showed his love for us,
  we too should love one another.
  For God has never been seen by anyone,
  but if we love each other, God dwells in us
  and God's love is fulfilled in us.
  And this is how we know that we dwell in God
    and God in us,
  in that God has given us a share in the Spirit.

1 John 4.11–13 JW

Alleluia, blessed are you who offer us life in abundance,
  alleluia.

See how good and pleasant it is for
brothers and sisters to dwell together in unity!

Like oil on the head that runs down on the beard, the
  beard of Aaron,
and on down to the edge of his garment;

or like the dew of Hermon raining down on the hills of Zion;
for that is the place our God blessed,
with the blessing of life for evermore.   *Psalm 133 JW*

Love in us, dear God,
that your Spirit be not quenched in us.
Love in us, so that we do not flag in loving.
Love in us, so that your world may share
the infinite abundance of your loving.

Well, then, if being in Christ brings any encouragement, any
motive for love and fellowship of spirit, any strong sense of
compassion, complete my joy by being of one mind, sharing the
same love, sympathy and unity of thinking, not acting out of
rivalry or ambition, but modestly, each one putting others ahead
of themselves, each looking not to their own interests but to
those of others.   *Philippians 2.1–5 jw*

Remember that God's love for the world
can overflow to all things only through lives
    where it dwells.
Remember that God feeds us with God's own life.
Let us be generous in recognizing that love
in surprising places, for Christ is not bound by us.
Let the whole world grow to its fulfilment
in the many-patterned beauty of love's design.

Joy of heaven, to earth come down!   *Charles Wesley*

Friday Morning Prayer

Alleluia, blessed are you, O God,
you burst the gates of death, alleluia.

> I will wipe away all tears from their eyes:
> and there will be no more death,
> neither sorrow, nor crying,
> neither shall there be any more pain,
> for the former things have passed away.

From Revelation 21.3–4

Alleluia, blessed are you, O God,
you burst the gates of death, alleluia.

While I felt secure, I said,
   'I shall never be disturbed.
You, O God, with your favour,
   made me as strong as the mountains.'

Then you hid your face,
and I was filled with fear.

I cried to you, O God;
I pleaded with you, saying,
'What profit is there in my blood,
   if I go down to the Pit?
Will the dust praise you or declare your faithfulness?

'Hear, O God, and have mercy upon me;
O God, be my helper.'

You have turned my wailing into dancing;
you have put off my sack-cloth and clothed me with joy;

Therefore my heart sings to you without ceasing;
O God my God, I will give you thanks for ever.   *Psalm 30.7–13*

Christ the Daystar,
dawn in our hearts
and dispel the shades of night.

On this mountain the Lord of hosts will make for all peoples
a feast of rich food, a feast of well-matured wines,
of rich food filled with marrow, of well-matured wines
strained clear.
And he will destroy on this mountain
the shroud that is cast over all peoples,
the sheet that is spread over all nations;
he will swallow up death for ever.
Then the Lord God will wipe away the tears from all faces.
Isaiah 25.6–8a

God of Paradox,
with our minds we know that death is not the end;
help us to believe it with our hearts and live it in our lives.
We pray for individuals and nations
living through dark times;
may they know soon the power of your resurrection.

I saw that God is our clothing – for love he enwraps us, embraces
us, enfolds us in a tender love that will never abandon us.
Julian of Norwich

Friday Evening Prayer

Alleluia, Jesus, Lord of life, we greet you, alleluia.

> Now Christ is risen from the dead
> and become the first fruits of those who sleep.
> For since death came through one person,
> from one person also comes the resurrection from the dead.
> And through him we have access to this grace
>   in which we stand,
> rejoicing in our hope of sharing the glory of God.
>
> *1 Corinthians 15.20, 21a; Romans 5.2 JW*

Alleluia, Jesus, Lord of life, we greet you, alleluia.

O God, you are my shepherd, and there is nothing I lack.
In a place of green pasture you make my dwelling.

With water and a resting place you tend me;
you restore my soul.

You guide me on paths of righteousness
for the sake of your name.

For if I pass through the midst of death's shadow,
I will not fear any ill, for you are with me,
your crook and your staff encourage me.

You set a table before me in the presence of my oppressors;
you have anointed my head with oil,
and the cup you give me is full of the best wine.

Your merciful love will follow me all the days of my life,
and my dwelling place will be in your house, O God, for ever.

Psalm 23 jw

God, give us courage to sit lightly to all that perishes,
and to reach out confidently towards the goal we cannot see,
in the power of your promised Spirit.

So then, my dear friends, just as you have always taken notice
of me, not just in my presence but now far more in my absence,
with fear and trembling work out your own salvation, for it is
God who is at work in you so that you both will and work in
ways that please him. Do everything without grumbling or argu-
ment – so you will become blameless and without fault, children
of God unstained in the midst of a crooked and perverse generation, where you shine like stars in the cosmos. Hold onto the
word of life, and I will be able to boast on the day of Christ
that I did not run in vain or labour vainly. Even if my life is
poured out in sacrifice and service of your faith, I am overjoyed
and rejoice with you all. In the same way you yourselves can be
overjoyed and rejoice with me.   *Philippians 2.12–18 jw*

Jesus, Gateway to fullness of life in God,
may our joy at your resurrection overflow
in service to those who suffer
from others' disapproval, persecution or oppression.
And may the Holy Spirit breathe through
the actions and lives of us all.

Easter

From the waiting comes the sign –
  come, Holy Spirit, come,
from the Presence comes the peace –
  come, Holy Spirit, come,
from the silence comes the song –
  come, Holy Spirit, come
and be to us, in truth,
  the sign, the peace, the song.

Shirley Erena Murray

Saturday Morning Prayer

Alleluia, blessed be God, soaring Spirit,
brooding over the universe, alleluia.

> A new heart I will give you,
> and a new spirit I will put within you;
> you shall be my people,
> and I will be your God.   *Ezekiel 36.26, 28*

Alleluia, blessed be God, soaring Spirit,
brooding over the universe, alleluia.

You send forth your spirit and they are created;
and so you renew the face of the earth.

May your glory, O God, endure for ever;
may you rejoice in all your works.

You look at the earth and it trembles;
you touch the mountains and they smoke.

I will sing to God as long as I live;
I will praise my God while I have my being.

Bless the Holy One, O my soul.
Alleluia!   *Psalm 104.31–34, 37*

> Christ the Daystar,
> dawn in our hearts
> and dispel the shades of night.

We know that the whole creation has been groaning in labour pains until now; and not only the creation, but we ourselves, who have the first fruits of the Spirit, groan inwardly while we wait for adoption, the redemption of our bodies. For in hope we were saved. Now hope that is seen is not hope. For who hopes for what is seen? But if we hope for what we do not see, we wait for it with patience.

Likewise the Spirit helps us in our weakness; for we do not know how to pray as we ought, but that very Spirit intercedes with sighs too deep for words. And God, who searches the heart, knows what is the mind of the Spirit, because the Spirit intercedes for the saints according to the will of God.

Romans 8.22–27

Come, Holy Spirit,
breathe life into our weary world;
illuminate the darkness of suffering,
that we may rejoice in the freshness of each new day.

Spirit of blessings, shine on our company.
Spirit of darkness, weave in us your new creation.
Spirit of weakness, empower us.
Spirit of justice, challenge us.
Spirit of peace, make us the messengers of your peace.
Spirit of the Living God who makes all things new,
Holy Spirit, come! *Mary Ann Ebert*

Saturday Evening Prayer

Alleluia, come, Holy Spirit,
enkindle your fire in our hearts, alleluia.

> Jesus breathed on his disciples and said,
> 'Receive the Holy Spirit.
> As the Father sent me, so I send you.'
> And the disciples were filled with joy
> and with the Holy Spirit.
> Jews and Greeks alike received the Spirit,
> and the disciples were filled with joy.

Alleluia, come, Holy Spirit,
enkindle your fire in our hearts, alleluia.

The Holy One, the God of gods, has spoken,
and called the earth from the rising of the sun to its setting.
From Zion God comes in majesty and beauty.

God, our God, you will come and manifest yourself,
    you will not keep silence;
fire blazes before you and a great storm around you.

You summon as witnesses the heavens above, and the earth,
for your judgement of your people.

Your people gather before you,
those who made the covenant with you with sacrifice,

and the heavens proclaim your righteousness,
that you, our God, are judge.   *Psalm 50.1–6 JW*

If we want to live by the Spirit,
let us seek the fruits of the Spirit:
love, joy, peace,
patience, kindness, goodness,
faithfulness, gentleness, self-control.
And if we live by the Spirit,
let us also be guided by the Spirit.

Jesus instructed his disciples, 'Do not leave Jerusalem, but await the Father's promise, about which you have heard from me: for John baptized with water, but you will be baptized with the Holy Spirit in very few days.' Then those gathered asked him, 'Master, are you going to restore the kingdom of Israel at this time?' He replied to them, 'It is not for you to know the times and seasons that the Father has kept in his own hands, but you will receive power when the Holy Spirit comes upon you, and you will be my witnesses in Jerusalem and in all Judea and Samaria and to the ends of the earth.'   *Acts 1.4–9 JW*

Great and marvellous are your works, O God,
and just and true your ways!
In the love of Jesus, born and living among us,
crucified and risen from the dead,
we invoke once more, and always,
your Holy Spirit:

In the burning is the fire –
   come, Holy Spirit, come,
in the spending is the gift –
   come, Holy Spirit, come,
in the breaking is the life –
   come, Holy Spirit, come
and be to us, in faith,
   the fire, the gift, the life.   *Shirley Erena Murray*

Sources and acknowledgements

Unless otherwise indicated, material from the Psalms is adapted from the *Book of Common Prayer* (1979) of The Episcopal Church in the USA, on which no copyright is claimed. Other biblical material, unless otherwise indicated, is from the New Revised Standard Version of the Bible, Anglicized Edition, copyright © 1989, 1995 by the Division of Christian Education of the National Council of the Churches of Christ in the USA. Used by permission. All rights reserved.

Extracts from the Bible marked NJB are excerpts from THE NEW JERUSALEM BIBLE, copyright © 1985 by Darton, Longman & Todd, Ltd and Doubleday, a division of Random House, Inc. Reprinted by Permission. The version of The Lord's Prayer in the Midday Prayer of Saturday is adapted from the English translation © English Language Liturgical Consultation (ELLC), 1988, and used by permission. See: www.englishtexts.org. Those passages marked JW are translations from the Greek by Jennifer Wild, © Jennifer Wild.

All material in the text without a source has been written by the authors, © Hannah Ward and Jennifer Wild.

In what follows, the details of sources are given in chronological order within each week; MP, EP and NP are abbreviations of Morning Prayer, Evening Prayer and Night Prayer.

Ordinary Time

Sunday MP: Mechthild of Magdeburg (*c.*1220–*c.*1280), in Brian Pickett (ed. and tr.), *The Heart of Love: Prayers of German Women Mystics* (London: St Paul Publications, 1991), p. 84, used by permission; Hildegard of Bingen (1098–1179), from *Symphonia*, tr. Jennifer Wild.

Monday MP: Hildegard of Bingen, from *Symphonia*, tr. Jennifer Wild.

Tuesday MP: Hildegard of Bingen, from *Symphonia*, tr. Jennifer Wild.

Thursday MP: John G. Whittier (1807–92), from his hymn 'Immortal love, forever full'.

Thursday EP: George Herbert (1593–1633), from *Love (III)*.

Saturday MP: John Keble (1792–1866), from the hymn 'New every morning', words from Keble's poem, 'Hues of the Rich Unfolding Morn', in *The Christian Year*, 1827.

Saturday EP: Julian of Norwich (*c.*1342–after 1416), *Showings*, ch. 5, tr. Jennifer Wild.

Night Prayer

Tuesday NP: Alexander Carmichael (comp. and ed.), *Carmina Gadelica: Hymns and Incantations Collected in the Highlands and Island of Scotland in the Last Century* (Edinburgh: Floris Books, 1992), p. 58.

Wednesday NP: adapted from Carmichael (comp. and ed.), *Carmina Gadelica*, p. 94.

Saturday NP: Carmichael (comp. and ed.), *Carmina Gadelica*, p. 36.

Advent

Sunday–Saturday MP: Dorothy McRae-McMahon, 'In weakness', in *Echoes of Our Journey: Liturgies of the People* (Melbourne: The Joint Board of Christian Education, 1993), p. 88, used by permission.

Sunday MP: Julian of Norwich, *Showings*, ch. 51, tr. Jennifer Wild.

Sunday EP: Traditional Advent Antiphon, version by Jennifer Wild.

Monday EP: Traditional Advent Antiphon, version by Jennifer Wild.

Tuesday MP: Kate McIlhagga, from 'Pregnant with Hope' in *The Green Heart of the Snowdrop* (Glasgow: Wild Goose Publications, 2004). © D. McIlhagga, 2004; used by permission.

Tuesday EP: Traditional Advent Antiphon, version by Jennifer Wild.

Wednesday EP: Traditional Advent Antiphon, version by Jennifer Wild.

Thursday MP: Julian of Norwich, *Showings*, ch. 4, tr. Jennifer Wild.

Thursday EP: Henry Vaughan (1621–95), from 'Religion'; traditional Advent Antiphon, version by Jennifer Wild.

Friday MP: McRae-McMahon, 'See the light', in *Echoes of Our Journey*, p. 76, used by permission.

Friday EP: Traditional Advent Antiphon, version by Jennifer Wild.

Saturday MP: Hadewijch of Antwerp (early thirteenth century), *The Complete Works*, Classics of Western Spirituality, tr. Mother Columba Hart OSB (New York: Paulist Press/London: SPCK, 1980), p. 197, used by permission.

Saturday EP: Traditional Advent Antiphon, version by Jennifer Wild.

Christmas

Sunday MP: Christina Rossetti (1830–94), from the hymn 'Love came down at Christmas', first published as a poem in her collection *Time Flies: A Reading Diary* (1885).

Sunday EP: Robert Herrick (1591–1674), refrain from his poem 'What sweeter music can we bring'.

Monday MP: Kate McIlhagga, 'Moontime of the winter', in *The Green Heart of the Snowdrop* (Glasgow: Wild Goose Publications, 2004). © D. McIlhagga, 2004; used by permission.

Tuesday MP: Richard Crashaw (*c*.1613–49), from his poem 'In the Holy Nativity of our Lord'.

Tuesday EP: George Herbert, from 'Trinity Sunday'.

Wednesday MP: Kate Compston, in *Bread of Tomorrow: Praying with the World's Poor*, ed. Janet Morley (London: SPCK and Christian Aid, 1992), p. 58, used by permission; Aelred of Rievaulx (1109–67), from Epiphany Sermon 3, tr. Jennifer Wild.

Wednesday EP: Irenaeus (*c*.130–*c*.200), from *Against Heresies*, 4, 20, 7, tr. Jennifer Wild.

Thursday EP: Christopher Smart (1722–71), from 'Hymn 32'; Augustine (354–430), *Confessions* 11.31, tr. Jennifer Wild; Barbara Reynolds, from the Introduction to *The Comedy of Dante Alighieri, the Florentine, Cantica III, Paradise (Il Paradiso)*, tr. Dorothy L. Sayers and Barbara Reynolds (London: Penguin Books, 1962).

Friday MP: Brian Wren, reproduced from 'Joyful is the dark', in *Piece Together Praise: A Theological Journey*, © 1996 Stainer & Bell Ltd, London, England, <www.stainer.co.uk>; used by permission.

Friday EP: Shirley Erena Murray, from 'Peace Child', no. 83 in *In Every Corner Sing: The Hymns of Shirley Erena Murray*, words: Shirley Erena Murray, © 1992 Hope Publishing Company, Carol Stream, IL 60188, <www.hopepublishing.com>. All rights reserved. Used by permission.

Saturday MP: Kate McIlhagga, 'Itching Ears', in *The Green Heart of the Snowdrop* (Glasgow: Wild Goose Publications, 2004). © D. McIlhagga, 2004; used by permission.

Lent

Sunday MP: Julian of Norwich, *Showings*, ch. 68, tr. Jennifer Wild.

Sunday EP: Gerard Manley Hopkins (1844–89), from 'Hope holds to Christ'.

Monday MP: Hosea 6.3 from *The Daily Office SSF* 1992 © The European Province of the Society of St Francis 1992; Carmichael (comp. and ed.), *Carmina Gadelica*, p. 47.

Monday EP: Augustine, *Confessions* 4.16, tr. Jennifer Wild.

Tuesday MP: Origin unknown, but often attributed to Brigid of Ireland (died *c.*523).

Wednesday MP: Anon.: the hymn is usually known as 'St Patrick's Breastplate', possibly eighth century.

Thursday MP: Cuthbert of Lindisfarne (died 687), in Bede, *Life of Cuthbert*, ch. 8, tr. Jennifer Wild.

Thursday EP: Augustine, from Sermon 272, tr. Jennifer Wild.

Friday MP: Brian Wren, reproduced from 'God of many names', in *Piece Together Praise: A Theological Journey*, © 1996 Stainer & Bell Ltd, London, England, <www.stainer.co.uk>; used by permission.

Friday EP: Thomas Traherne (1637–74), The First Century, no. 58 in *Centuries*.

Saturday EP: Henry Vaughan, from 'The Dawning'.

Easter

Sunday MP: Carmichael (comp. and ed.), *Carmina Gadelica*, p. 280.

Sunday EP: John Chrysostom (*c.*347–407), from his Easter homily, tr. Jennifer Wild.

Monday MP: Carmichael (comp. and ed.), *Carmina Gadelica*, p. 286.

Monday EP: Charles Wesley (1707–88), from the hymn 'Christ the Lord is risen today' (sometimes the first verse is given as 'Love's redeeming work is done').

Tuesday MP: McRae-McMahon, 'Set us free', in *Echoes of Our Journey*, p. 83, used by permission.

Wednesday MP: Janet Morley, in Hannah Ward, Jennifer Wild and Janet Morley (eds), *Celebrating Women: The New Edition* (London: SPCK, 1995), p. 149, used by permission.

Thursday EP: Charles Wesley, from the hymn 'Love divine, all loves excelling'.

Friday MP: Julian of Norwich, *Showings*, ch. 5, tr. Jennifer Wild.

Friday EP: Shirley Erena Murray, from 'From the waiting comes the sign', no. 24 in *In Every Corner Sing: The Hymns of Shirley Erena Murray*, words:

Shirley Erena Murray, © 1992 Hope Publishing Company, Carol Stream, IL 60188, <www.hopepublishing.com>. All rights reserved. Used by permission.

Saturday MP: Mary Ann Ebert, in Hannah Ward and Jennifer Wild (eds), *The Way of Peace* (Oxford: Lion, 1999), p. 56, © P. A. E. Ebert; used by permission.

Saturday EP: Shirley Erena Murray, from 'From the waiting comes the sign', no. 24 in *In Every Corner Sing: The Hymns of Shirley Erena Murray*, words: Shirley Erena Murray, © 1992 Hope Publishing Company, Carol Stream, IL 60188, <www.hopepublishing.com>. All rights reserved. Used by permission.

Printed in Great Britain
by Amazon.co.uk, Ltd.,
Marston Gate.